CURRENCY RISK MANAGEMENT

SELECTED RESEARCH PAPERS

Editors

Dr. M.S.V. Prasad, M.Com. MBA, Ph.D.

Head - Department of Finance
GITAM Institute of Management
GITAM – Deemed to be University, Visakhapatnam

and

Dr. G.V. Satya Sekhar, MBA, Ph.D.

Associate Professor, Centre for Distance Learning
GITAM – Deemed to be University, Visakhapatnam

Conference Conducted by

Department of Finance

GITAM Institute of Management

GITAM – Deemed to be University, Visakhapatnam

Sponsored by

Indian Bank, Visakhapatnam

Series in Business and Finance

VERNON PRESS

www.vernonpress.com

In the Americas:
Vernon Press
1000 N West Street,
Suite 1200, Wilmington,
Delaware 19801
United States

In the rest of the world:
Vernon Press
C/Sancti Espiritu 17,
Malaga, 29006
Spain

Series in Business and Finance

Library of Congress Control Number: 2018961843

ISBN: 978-1-62273-677-5

Also available:

Hardback: 978-1-62273-443-6

E-book: 978-1-62273-569-3

Table of contents

List of tables

List of figures

Preface

Risk management is a combination of multiple ideas to control trading risk. It can be limiting trade lot size, hedging, trading only during certain hours or days, or knowing when to take losses. Currency Risk Management (CRM) can make the difference between the survival and sudden death of an organization which deals with Forex trading.

CRM is indispensable in the ever-changing global business environment. CRM's methodology is used in the banking sector to help enterprises. At present some software tools are providing a comprehensive hedging solution for risk management of companies. However, outsourcing the activities of CRM is an efficacious choice for small-scale and medium-scale business enterprises.

Currency Exchange (CX) transactions could be capital or revenue in nature. It is essential that companies which have exposure to foreign exchange should have a team in their treasury department for effective and expeditious management of exchange-risks. In a floating exchange rate environment, the currency exchange rate responds to the flow of imports and exports, the flow of capital, relative inflation rates and more. Often, limits are placed on currency exchange rate fluctuations according to government policies. There are different tools for hedging currency exchange risk, which includes forwards, futures, swaps and options.

Most currency management instruments enable the firm to take a long or a short position as a part of a hedging strategy. Some of these instruments are derivatives and have recently evolved.

In India, CX business is subject to RBI's rules and regulations, government guidelines and the Foreign Exchange Management Act (FEMA). Whatever may be the strategy the dealers always face severe losses in CX management.

'Currency Risk Management' needs the attention of academicians, bankers and the aspirant management students. Hence, a conference on 'Currency Risk Management' was organized by the Department of Finance, GITAM University, and Visakhapatnam, India in association with Indian Bank, Visakhapatnam, India. We have received qualitative responses from academicians and the following issues were addressed in the conference:

- India's shift to a market determined exchange rate regime and the impact of structural change.

- Consequences of unlimited geographical boundaries with relation to the foreign exchange market.

- Influence of 'Currency Futures' was introduced in August 2008 and their impact on hedgers to manage the risk arising out of increased volatility in exchange rate.

- Problems of the high volatility of exchange rates are a fact of life faced by every company engaged in International business, bringing in uncertainties in their bottom line.

- In recent years, variations in the value of rupee have been very impulsive and unpredictable. These fluctuations have had a profound impact on domestic and foreign sales, profit levels and profit margins of MNCs operating in India.

This book is an outcome in the form of 'conference proceedings from the national conference on currency risk management' and it contains selected research papers.

Acronyms of Currencies Across Globe

Country/Currency	Acronym/Abbreviation
Australia Dollar	AUD
Great Britain Pound	GBP
Euro	EUR
Japan Yen	JPY
Switzerland Franc	CHF
US Dollar	USD
Afghanistan Afghani	AFN
Albania Lek	ALL
Algeria Dinar	DZD
Angola Kwanza	AOA
Argentina Peso	ARS
Armenia Dram	AMD
Aruba Florin	AWG
Australia Dollar	AUD
Austria Schilling	ATS (EURO)
Belgium Franc	BEF (EURO)
Azerbaijan New Manat	AZN
Bahamas Dollar	BSD
Bahrain Dinar	BHD
Bangladesh Taka	BDT
Barbados Dollar	BBD
Belarus Ruble	BYR
Belize Dollar	BZD
Bermuda Dollar	BMD
Bhutan Ngultrum	BTN
Bolivia Boliviano	BOB
Bosnia Mark	BAM

Botswana Pula	BWP
Brazil Real	BRL
Great Britain Pound	GBP
Brunei Dollar	BND
Bulgaria Lev	BGN
Burundi Franc	BIF
CFA Franc BCEAO	XOF
CFA Franc BEAC	XAF
CFP Franc	XPF
Cambodia Riel	KHR
Canada Dollar	CAD
Cape Verde Escudo	CVE
Cayman Islands Dollar	KYD
Chili Peso	CLP
China Yuan/Renminbi	CNY
Colombia Peso	COP
Comoros Franc	KMF
Congo Franc	CDF
Costa Rica Colon	CRC
Croatia Kuna	HRK
Cuba Convertible Peso	CUC
Cuba Peso	CUP
Cyprus Pound	CYP (EURO)
Czech Koruna	CZK
Denmark Krone	DKK
Djibouti Franc	DJF
Dominican Republic Peso	DOP
East Caribbean Dollar	XCD
Egypt Pound	EGP
El Salvador Colon	SVC
Estonia Kroon	EEK (EURO)

Ethiopia Birr	ETB
Euro	EUR
Falkland Islands Pound	FKP
Finland Markka	FIM (EURO)
Fiji Dollar	FJD
Gambia Dalasi	GMD
Georgia Lari	GEL
German Mark	DMK (EURO)
Ghana New Cedi	GHS
Gibraltar Pound	GIP
Greece Drachma	GRD (EURO)
Guatemala Quetzal	GTQ
Guinea Franc	GNF
Guyana Dollar	GYD
Haiti Gourde	HTG
Honduras Lempira	HNL
Hong Kong Dollar	HKD
Hungary Forint	HUF
Iceland Krona	ISK
India Rupee	INR
Indonesia Rupiah	IDR
Iran Rial	IRR
Iraq Dinar	IQD
Ireland Pound	IED (EURO)
Israel New Shekel	ILS
Italy Lira	ITL (EURO)
Jamaica Dollar	JMD
Japan Yen	JPY
Jordan Dinar	JOD
Kazakhstan Tenge	KZT
Kenya Shilling	KES

Kuwait Dinar	KWD
Kyrgyzstan Som	KGS
Laos Kip	LAK
Latvia Lats	LVL (EURO)
Lebanon Pound	LBP
Lesotho Loti	LSL
Liberia Dollar	LRD
Libya Dinar	LYD
Lithuania Litas	LTL (EURO)
Luxembourg Franc	LUF (EURO)
Macau Pataca	MOP
Macedonia Dinar	MKD
Malagasy Ariary	MGA
Malawi Kwacha	MWK
Malaysia Ringgit	MYR
Maldives Rufiyaa	MVR
Malta Lira	MTL (EURO)
Mauritania Ouguiya	MRO
Mauritius Rupee	MUR
Mexico Peso	MXN
Moldova Leu	MDL
Mongolia Tugrik	MNT
Morocco Dirham	MAD
Mozambique New Metical	MZN
Myanmar Kyat	MMK
NL Antilles Guilder	ANG
Namibia Dollar	NAD
Nepal Rupee	NPR
Netherlands Guilder	NLG (EURO)
New Zealand Dollar	NZD
Nicaragua Cordoba Oro	NIO

Nigeria Naira	NGN
North Korea Won	KPW
Norway Kroner	NOK
Oman Rial	OMR
Pakistan Rupee	PKR
Panama Balboa	PAB
Papua New Guinea Kina	PGK
Paraguay Guarani	PYG
Peru Nuevo Sol	PEN
Philippines Peso	PHP
Poland Zloty	PLN
Portugal Escudo	PTE (EURO)
Qatar Rial	QAR
Romania New Lei	RON
Russia Ruble	RUB
Rwanda Franc	RWF
Samoa Tala	WST
Sao Tome/Principe Dobra	STD
Saudi Arabia Riyal	SAR
Serbia Dinar	RSD
Seychelles Rupee	SCR
Sierra Leone	SLL
Singapore Dollar	SGD
Slovakia Koruna	SKK (EURO)
Slovenia Tolar	SIT (EURO)
Solomon Islands Dollar	SBD
Somali Shilling	SOS
South Africa Rand	ZAR
South Korea Won	KRW
Spain Peseta	ESP (EURO)
Sri Lanka Rupee	LKR

St Helena Pound	SHP
Sudan Pound	SDG
Suriname Dollar	SRD
Swaziland Lilangeni	SZL
Sweden Krona	SEK
Switzerland Franc	CHF
Syria Pound	SYP
Taiwan Dollar	TWD
Tanzania Shilling	TZS
Thailand Baht	THB
Tonga Pa'anga	TOP
Trinidad/Tobago Dollar	TTD
Tunisia Dinar	TND
Turkish New Lira	TRY
Turkmenistan Manat	TMM
US Dollar	USD
Uganda Shilling	UGX
Ukraine Hryvnia	UAH
Uruguay Peso	UYU
United Arab Emirates Dirham	AED
Vanuatu Vatu	VUV
Venezuela Bolivar	VEB
Vietnam Dong	VND
Yemen Rial	YER
Zambia Kwacha	ZMK
Zimbabwe Dollar	ZWD

Abstracts

A Comparative Study of Forex Trade of India and China through Forecasting using Brown's Method

Kamakshaiah Musunuru,
Assistant Professor, Business Analytics,
GITAM School of International Business,
GITAM University, Visakhapatnam.
Mobile No.: +919177573730
Email: Kamakshaiah.m@gmail.com

Prof. S. S. Prasada Rao,
Dean, Academic Affairs,
GITAM University, Visakhapatnam.
Email: profsspr@gmail.com

This paper aims to find out whether the performance of currency markets is similar or not by giving due diligence to differences. Certain secondary data sources are analyzed in order to evaluate the hypothesis: 'the performance of currency is not the same'.

NSE data shows that the average daily turnover in currency futures market in FY16 stands at USD 2.5trillion, compared with Rs 12,705 crore for FY15. FOREX trade is allowed in India only through Multi Commodity Exchange (MCX- SX) National Stock Exchange (NSE) and SEBI only with few currency pairs. China's Forex market turnover surged, highlighting capital flight pressure, turnover jumped 42 percent to a record USD 2.32 trillion in 2016. Both countries are more or less similar in performance as far as currency trading is concerned with a wide variety of political, social and cultural dissimilarities.

Brown's model was used for forecasting the data. The model proved to be highly reliable by giving rise to more precise and accurate forecasting results.

Aim:

The aim of this study is to explore and compare the future status of the foreign exchange trade of both India and China. The research methodology is a comparative and exploratory study.

Objectives:

1. To study the present status of foreign exchange trade in India and China.

2. To find and fit an appropriate model that which can explain the present status of Forex trade.

3. To forecast the future status of the Forex trade.

Keywords:

Currency trading, Forex trade, Time series analysis, Forecasting, Brown's model

India's Exchange Traded Currency Derivatives Market: An Overview

Gangineni Dhananjhay,
Professor (Finance), MBA Department,
Narayana Engineering College, Nellore (A.P), 524004.
Mobile No.: 09391319721
Email: gdhananjhay@gmail.com

Prof. S. S. Prasada Rao,
Dean, Academic Affairs,
GITAM University, Visakhapatnam.
Email: profsspr@gmail.com

India's shift to a market determined exchange rate regime in 1993 was an important structural change. Extreme financial markets volatility has been witnessed in the last five years both internationally and domestically. Until 2008, only Over-the-Counter (OTC) contracts were available to hedge currency risk with banks as counterparties. Currency Futures were introduced in August 2008 to help hedgers manage the risk arising out of increased volatility in exchange rate. This helped market participants with the provision of an Exchange-Traded-Contract (ETC) with familiar features of Anonymous Electronic Consolidated Limit Order Book (AECLOB) Market with central clearing house resulting in higher transparency. This paper analyses the growth of currency derivatives segments in the major exchanges NSE, MCX-SX, and USE. The market share of various currency derivatives products was studied and conclusions were drawn for hedgers, speculators, market intermediaries and regulators of Forex market in India for ensuring effective currency market.

Objectives:

1. To examine the business growth of different currency derivative products at MCX-SX, NSE, USE, BSE.

2. To examine the market share of various currency derivative products.

Keywords:

Currency Derivatives, Trading, Volatility, International Finance, Forex Risk Management, NSE

An Overview of the Foreign Exchange Market in India

G.Santhoshi Kumari,
Assistant Professor,
Noble Institute of Science and Technology,
Visakhapatnam.
Email: santhoshigondesi@gmail.com

Dr.M.S.V. Prasad,
Associate Professor, Head,
Department of Finance,
GITAM Institute of Management,
GITAM University, Visakhapatnam.
Email: msv@gitam.edu

The foreign exchange market plays a significant role in global trade in determining the strength of an economy and its growth. It is also essential for international finance. The foreign exchange market India is growing rapidly. The annual turnover of the market is more than $400 billion. This transaction does not include the inter-bank transactions. The Indian foreign exchange market consists of buyers, sellers, market intermediaries and the monetary authority of India. The foreign exchange market is not limited by any geographical boundaries. It does not have any regular market timings because it operates 24 hours 7 days week 365 days a year. It is characterized by an ever-growing trading volume and exhibiting great heterogeneity among market participants with major institutional investor buying and selling millions of dollars at one go or a minor participant like an individual buying or selling less than 100 dollars.

The Foreign Exchange market in India operates under the Central Government of India and executes wide powers to control transactions in foreign exchange. The Foreign Exchange Management Act, 1999 or FEMA regulates the whole Foreign Exchange market in India.

Objectives:

1. To discuss the role of foreign exchange market in an economy.

2. To understand the Forex market, details about trading volume, market participants, and the different types of Forex products.

Keywords:

Foreign Exchange, Foreign Exchange Market, International Finance, FEMA

Pareto Currency Risk Management Strategy - A Passive Hedge

Dr.K. Bhanu Prakash,
Associate Professor,
V ESTAL Institutions, Eluru.
Mobile No.: +91-9440321648.

Dr. Chowdary Venu Gopal,
Assistant Professor,
GITAM University, Bengaluru.
Mobile No.: +91-9440710959
Email: drchowdary959@gmail.com

The Indian Rupee (INR) is pegged, on the rebound and is expected to remain range bound at 64.3 against the US$ in the current FY and is likely to be lower at 65.4 in 2018-19. INR has been among the better performing currencies in the emerging markets according to the UBS Report. EUR-INR is expected to trade higher, a 10-Year Indian benchmark yield of 6.0-6.3 percent range and is moving higher on inflation expectations. With Sterling fluctuations, Britain's Pound see-sawed and the Swiss Franc fell to its lowest level in over 2-Years against the Euro. In every facet of Global Currency Market volatility pervades, uncertainty persists, complexity perplexes and ambiguity penetrates. Hence, an attempt has been made to evaluate hedging policies to mitigate currency risk in general and Pareto Currency Risk Management Strategy, a passive hedge in specific. It is also suggested that the passive and smart hedging policies are used for improving financial stability over time in a fragile currency world.

Objectives:

1. To understand various currency risk management strategies.

2. To analyze the Pareto currency risk management strategy.

A Study on Price Discovery of Currency Futures at NSE

Satyanarayana Koilada,
Assistant professor,
Noble Institute of Science and Technology,
Lankelapalem, Visakhapatnam.
Email: justsatya@gmail.com

Haniefuddin Sk,
Director,
Noble Institute of Science and Technology,
Lankelapalem, Visakhapatnam.
Email: haniefuddin@rediffmail.com

The foreign exchange market is the world's largest market in terms of trade value. It is important to note that as the market is growing bigger, foreign exchange management is gaining significance. Currency derivatives are very useful tools for traders and can be used as a tool for mitigating future exchange rate risk. Currency derivatives at NSE available on USD/INR are most traded currency derivatives in the world for the year 2016-17 after USD/RUB futures that are traded on the Moscow Exchange. Since the currency futures market facilitates an advantage for the investor through marginal investment.

Granger Causality Test is used for identifying the lead-lag relationship between the currency spot and futures markets. We have identified the currency future rates lead spot rates for USD/INR, GBR/INR and EURO/INR currency pairs. We have considered daily closing rates for NSE currency futures and currency spot rates for selected pairs of currencies i.e. USD/INR, GBP/INR, JPY/INR and EURO/INR. It is found that the spot rate for JPY/INR leads the future rate. It is also identified that the spot rate for USD/INR does not cause changes in futures rate.

The variance decomposition technique applied for each vector autoregressive (VAR) model estimated separately for each currency pair data sampled from spot and futures market. It is found that there is almost no impact of variance in USD/INR spot rate on future rate variance which signifies the market for USD/INR is strong and matured compared to the markets for remaining currency pairs.

Objectives:

1. To examine the relationship between the NSE currency future rates and currency spot rates in order to identify the price discovery mechanism.

2. To study the relationship between at NSE market and its integration with foreign exchange market.

Exchange Rate Risk in the Foreign Exchange Market:
A Challenge on Corporate Profitability

Tejswini Basatry,
Research Scholar,
GITAM Institute of Management,
GITAM University, Visakhapatnam.

Prof. P. Sheela, MBA, Ph.D.,
Principal,
GITAM Institute of Management,
GITAM University, Visakhapatnam.

The foreign exchange market is the largest traded market across the globe. In India, the foreign exchange market opened for trade during the 1970's and most of the transactions were done through banks. Many companies in India emerged as global players during this period. However, they need to face the exchange rate risk of volatility in the global trade as the exchange rate against US dollar has raised five folds during this period. Importantly the risk exposure of Indian companies to its foreign trade has also increased dramatically. Conceptually, the foreign exchange market faces risks of transaction exposure, translation exposure, and operating exposure which seem to be part of the exchange rate determination system. The hedging measures to be part of the risk management practices in the foreign exchange system across the global market.

As the exchange rate has challenged Indian corporate at many periods of interval, due to which volatile movement of exchange rate directly impact the corporate profitability. Infosys risk hedging is being analyzed to know how it manages the exchange risk volatility and the impact on corporate profitability is studied with reference to information technology (IT) industry. The historical picture of the exchange rate of INR against major currencies like US Dollar, Euro, Pound sterling, and Yen, surprised many corporate entities and had a direct impact on the corporate profit.

This paper brings out the problem of exchange rate risk and its effect on corporate profitability in the IT industry.

Objectives:

1. To study the impact of fluctuations in foreign exchange on corporate profitability.

2. To know how to manage the exchange risk volatility and impact on corporate profitability is studied with reference to information technology (IT) industry.

Keywords:

Corporate Profitability, Exchange Rate, Foreign Exchange Market, Risk, Volatility

Forex Exchange Management and Challenges
in Current Global Economic Environment

Dr. Shamshuddin Shaik,
Assistant Professor, GITAM University.
Mobile No.: +91-8019716116
Email: shamshuddin1234@gmail.com

Dr. Shaik Khadar Baba,
Andhra University.
Mobile No.: +91-9989570027
Email: skkbaba@yahoo.com

Dr. Haniefuddin Shaik,
Director NISTV.
Email: haniefuddin@rediffmail.com

'Forex market' in general is the market in which currencies are traded. The Forex market is one of the largest liquid markets in the world, with normal traded values amounting to trillions of dollars per day. Forex market includes all of the currencies in the world. Government intervention in the foreign exchange market is inevitable when the authority is vested with some intentions to which the intervention policy is vested. RBI maintains Forex reserves as the prime objective following the balance of payment crises that surfaced during the year 1990-1991. The demand for reserve arises because exchange rate intervention which is largely conducted in the form of buying and selling of reserves in the market for which the authority needs to maintain sufficient amount of reserves.

Demand for reserves tends to be inversely related to the flexibility of managed float and more rigid when the system reserve is required.

Objectives:

1. To study the challenges and trends of Forex management in India.

2. To analyze the role of exchange rate regimes.

Assessment of Operational Risk Management -
Global vs Local Banking Sector

Dr.G.V.Satya Sekhar,
Associate Professor,
GITAM (Deemed to be University),
Visakhapatnam.

Dr.N.R.Mohan Prakash,
Assistant Professor,
GITAM (Deemed to be University),
Visakhapatnam.

The banking sector is now facing a challenging task to cope with operational risk management. The most used operational risk examples involve: system break-downs or system errors; a transactions' process or a control of errors; the activity stop; internal or external criminal acts; security disrespect or staff risks; improper control at all levels; the inexistence of the responsibility and of regulations for an integrated system, which can record data wrongly for a long period of time.

The banking risks are a source of unexpected expenses; proper manage-ment can stabilize the incomes in time by lessening the damage caused. At the same time, the consolidation of the banking shares' value can be made through real communication with financial markets and the implementation of proper programs to administrate banking risks.

In this chapter, special attention is given to identify the effects of operation-al risk from external sources; it is because improper information can expose the financial institution to very important operational risks. The operational risks can affect the institution solvency and can generate a wrong approach of the consumers and also a fall of trust for the banking market.

Objectives:

1. To appraise operational risk management in the banking sec-tor in India.

2. To make a comparative analysis of global and local banking systems.

Keywords:

Operational Risk Management, Reputation Risk Management, Basel II and III norms

Foreign Exchange Risk Management Practices
in Commercial Banks of India

Koneru Kusuma,
Assistant Professor,
GITAM Institute of Management,
GITAM University.

V.Gowri Lakshmi,
Assistant Professor,
GITAM Institute of Management,
GITAM University.

The purpose of this study is to explore different aspects of foreign exchange risk management by the commercial banks of India. This study tries to explore different characteristics of net foreign currency exposure practices and tools used by commercial banks in this regard and income from foreign currencies of commercial banks. The role of commercial banks in foreign exchange risk management: they should merge their money market and foreign exchange operations and treat them as a separate profit centre for better efficiency, foreign exchange derivatives market contracts, overseas commodity, freight hedging, rupee accounts of nonresident banks, interbank foreign exchange dealings are governed by the provisions in notifications.

Objectives:

1. To study the foreign exchange risk concept in commercial banks

2. To enumerate various techniques and tools used to mitigate foreign exchange risk management in commercial banks of India

3. To evaluate the role of central bank in foreign exchange risk management by the commercial banks of India

Keywords:

Risk, Exposure, Net assets, Foreign currency, Commercial banks

Chapter 1

A Comparative Study of Forex Trade of India and China through Forecasting using Brown's Method

Kamakshaiah Musunuru,
Assistant Professor, Business Analytics,
GITAM School of International Business,
GITAM University, Visakhapatnam.
Mobile No.: +919177573730
Email: Kamakshaiah.m@gmail.com

Prof. S. S. Prasada Rao,
Dean, Academic Affairs,
GITAM University, Visakhapatnam.
Email: profsspr@gmail.com

Introduction

Currency trading is the act of buying and selling international currencies. Very often, banks and financial trading institutions engage in the act of currency trading. Individual investors can also engage in currency trading, attempting to benefit from variations in the exchange rate of the currencies. The currency trading (FOREX) market is the biggest and the fastest growing market in the world economy. Its daily turnover is more than 2.5 trillion dollars, which is 100 times greater than the NASDAQ daily turnover. Every day more than USD 3 trillion in currencies change hands in a highly professional interbank market, in which electronic trading platforms link currency traders from banks across the world directly. FOREX markets are effectively open 24 hours a day, thanks to global cooperation among currency traders.

Factors that affect the foreign exchange market

Interest rates, inflation, and GDP are the main variables; however, other economic indicators such as unemployment rate, BOP, trade deficit, fiscal deficit, manufacturing indices, consumer prices, and retail sales amongst others. News and information regarding a country's economy can have a direct impact on the direction that the country's currency is heading in much the same way that current events and financial news affect stock prices, so the importance of economic factors. The following eight economic factors will directly affect a currency's movements in the Forex market. Interest rates, inflation, and GDP numbers are the main variables; however, other economic indicators such as unemployment rate, bop, trade deficit, fiscal deficit, manufacturing indices, consumer prices and retail sales are among others.

News and information regarding a country's economy can have a direct impact on the direction that the country's currency is heading in much the same way that current events and financial news affect stock prices, hence the importance of economic factors.

Any resident Indian or company including banks and financial institutions can participate in the futures market. However, at present, Foreign Institutional Investors (FIIs) and Non-Resident Indians (NRIs) are not permitted to participate in currency futures market. Any currency can be traded on the international level. However, on the Multi Commodity Exchange (MCX- SX), only four major currencies are traded against the Indian Rupee.

- USDINR

- EURINR

- GBPINR

- JPYINR

The commonly used exchanges on the national level are - Multi Commodity Exchange (MCX- SX) and National Stock Exchange (NSE). The most commonly used exchange on the international level - COMEX who are the Regulator of the Market. The currency market is regulated jointly by the Reserve Bank of India (RBI), and Securities and Exchange Board of India (SEBI).

What is a margin? Margin is a performance bond that ensures against trading losses. Margin requirements in the FOREX marketplace allow one to hold positions larger than the asset value of one's account. Trading with Forex Capital Management includes a pre-trade check for margin availability; the trade is executed only if there are sufficient margin funds in one's account. The Forex Capital Management trading system calculates cash on hand necessary to cover current positions, and provides this information to users in real time. If funds in your account fall below margin requirements, the system will close all open positions. This prevents your account from falling below your available equity, which is a key protection in this volatile, fast-moving marketplace.

Literature Review

Suresh (2012) studied the exchange rate impact on bilateral trade between India and China. The study mentions that China and India had similar development strategies prior to the breaking out of their deliberate insulation from the world economy and the ushering in of market-oriented economic reforms and liberalization. China began reforming its closed, centrally planned, non-market economy in 1978. India always had a large private sector and functioning markets, which were subject to rigid state controls until the hesitant and piecemeal reforms of the 1980s. Since the study is empirical, the paper concludes that the revaluation of RMB will have an impact on the trade of India, particularly with higher elasticity for imports.

McCauley and Scatigna (2011) predict FOREX turnover against certain variables such as income, which augments financial depth, complexity and openness. The study concludes that the association of higher interest rates with higher turnover suggests that relatively high inflation, among other causes of relatively high nominal yields, can attract perhaps unwanted attention in a world with low yields in the main economies.

Fratzscher and Mehl (2011) assessed whether the international monetary system is already tri-polar and centered on the US dollar, the euro and the Chinese renminbi (RMB). The study focuses on what we call China's "dominance hypothesis", i.e. whether the renminbi is already the dominant currency in Asia, exerting a large influence on exchange rate and monetary policies in the region, a direct reference to the old "German dominance hypothesis" which ascribed to the German mark a dominant role in Europe in the 1980s-1990s. Using a global factor model of exchange rates and a complementary event study, the study finds evidence that the RMB has become a key driver of currency movements in emerging Asia since the mid-2000s, and even more so since the global financial crisis. These results are consistent with China's dominance hypothesis and with the view that the international monetary system has already been tri-polar. However, they also find that China's currency movements are to some extent affected by those in the rest of Asia.

Patnaik and Shah (2009) studied the difficulties of the Chinese and Indian exchange rate regimes. The study identifies several features and similarities in FOREX trading. The study mentions that both countries implemented dollar pegs through sterilized intervention in an environment of substantial restrictions against capital flows. However, the key argument of this paper seems to be the policy framework has induced substantial difficulties, and imposed significant costs upon both economies. The study also identifies issues such as durability, mismatch, and a few others that makes the trade little distinct from each other.

Ito et al., (2008) analyse the relationships between the unit of account and means of exchange functions of an international currency, on the one hand, and its store of value in official use, on the other. The study mentions that the historical evidence links the currency composition of reserves to currency movements. The study also finds that the currency composition of reserves is strongly related in the cross-section to both currency movements and the currency denomination of trade. The study finds data limitations making it hard to distinguish these two factors. A panel analysis of 5 countries from central and Eastern Europe shows that both trade invoicing and currency movements drive changing official reserve composition. Implications are suggested for the prospects for the renminbi enlarging its current small portion of official foreign exchange reserves.

Research Methods

Problem statement

The aim of the study is to study the present status of forex trade and make future predictions. The present forex trade in the world is very volatile. This is very much akin to a few of the ASEAN countries such as Afghanistan, Bangladesh, India, Pakistan, China, etc. The performance of these countries with respect to foreign exchange trade is precarious and dire. Though international economics are so auspicious about the situation, the context is hopeless as the currency values are falling drastically with a significant upward trend. This means the number of currency units under exchange by few countries such as India and China are drastically increasing against the US and the UK. This shows a very steep upward trend in the foreign exchange trade. However, this would be an auspicious trend for those engaging in trading with the US and the UK currencies. This leads indirectly to the loss of trade to countries like India and China as the currencies are out-valued compared to developed countries. This is, in fact, rudimentary input for this study which serves as a statement of the problem.

Data sources

This research employs secondary data analysis. The data is obtained from the WTO repository. There are other valid repositories with the same data.[1] For instance, OECD maintains a huge repository for foreign exchange and

---

[1] Please visit https://data.gov.in/catalog/foreign-exchange-reserves-year-wise for more detail on data sets for foreign exchange.

currency valuations.[2] So, the data sets were publicly available and highly precise for academic and corporate research needs. The data set used for this study is a time series data with 54 records and 3 fields. Each record is represented by year against the name of the country, currency exchange for India and China as filed names.

The hypothesis of the study is as follows:

H_1: *India and China are significantly different with respect to FOREX trade*

The Box-Ljung Test is required to test autocorrelations which is one of the prerequisites to forecasting. Box-Ljung Test is useful to evaluate autocorrelations whether they are significant or not. The test statistic is:

$$Q = n(n+2) \sum_{k=1}^{h} \frac{\rho_k^2}{n-k}$$

Q is the test statistic, n is the sample size, k is the lag operator, ρ is the sample estimate of the autocorrelation. During this stage the Box-Ljung Test employs a hypothesis.

H_0: *the data is independently distributed (identically independent distribution)*

Box-Ljung Test statistic is useful to evaluate whether the serial correlations i.e. autocorrelations are really significant or not. The test statistic for sufficient sample size is approximately equal to $\chi^2_{(1-\alpha),h}$ i.e., chi-square distribution with α quartile and h degrees of freedom: $\chi^2_{(1-\alpha),h}$.

This test statistic is very sensitive to sample size so with a degree of freedom.

Of course, the other important issue in modeling time series on time bound data is the model. Brown's model is used in this study. There are many models such as Holt, Winter's, Prais Winsten, Cochrane Orcutt to name a few. Brown's model, which belongs to exponential smoothing, is very simple yet robust in modeling and forecasting data. The model is assumed to be linear yet seasonal. Brown's model appears in two special contexts in time series analysis and forecasting viz., first, the basic time series forecasting and secondly double exponential smoothing. The expression for basic time series forecasting is as follows:

$$S_t = \alpha.x_t + (1-\alpha).S_{t-1}$$

WhereS_t the series at time t. 'α' is the smoothing parameter for the forecasting. S_{t-1} is the series at lag 1. The above expression is a very simple form of the basic exponential smoothing. However, the double parameter exponential

---

[2] Please visit https://data.oecd.org/conversion/exchange-rates.htm for more details on data sets for foreign exchange and currency valuation.

smoothing which is proposed by the Brown is different. The forecast beyond x_t can be expressed as follows:

$$S'_t = \alpha x_t + (1 - \alpha)S'_{t-1}$$
$$S''_t = \alpha S_t + (1 - \alpha)S''_{t-1}$$

The general form for the above equations is:

$$F_t = \alpha_t + m\beta_t$$

Where

$$\alpha_t = 2S_t + S''_t$$
$$\beta_t = \frac{\alpha}{1 - \alpha} + (S_t - S''_t)$$

As a matter of evaluation there are certain fit indices to assess the forecasting model. The foremost index is R^2 measure, which is:

$$R^2 = 1 - \frac{SS_{reg}}{SS_{tot}}$$

Where SS_{reg} : represents regression error or sum of squares for fitted or regressed values.

SS_{tot} : represents total sum of squares. This index helps to assess the fitness of the model. Usually, the R^2 value shows the percentage of error in regression explained by the total error in the model. This value needs to be reasonably high and close to one. However, there is much suspicion that R^2 is not a reasonable measure to assess the fit. That is why; there is a plethora of other measures or indices that help to check that whether the fit is reasonably well or not. Other measures include RMSE, MAPE, MAE, AIC, and BIC. This measure serves for rechecking of the results obtained using regression model.

Analysis

As it was mentioned in the research methods, the primary aim of this study is to compare and evaluate the present and future of the forex trade in India and China. The analysis of this study has two parts. The data sets first analyzed by ACF and PACF in order to evaluate autocorrelations. This helps to determine which model needs to be selected for forecasting. The second part performs the model and tests the same for forecasting. The model chosen is evaluated against the actual and fitted values through certain measures.

Part 1: Autocorrelations

1.1. China

Table 1.1: Autocorrelations for China FOREX data. Series: China.

Lag	Autocorrelation	Std. Error[a]	Box-Ljung Statistic		
			Value	df	Sig.[b]
1	.973	.129	56.849	1	.000
2	.943	.128	111.176	2	.000
3	.909	.127	162.589	3	.000
4	.868	.126	210.356	4	.000
5	.816	.124	253.433	5	.000
6	.761	.123	291.641	6	.000
7	.702	.122	324.829	7	.000
8	.641	.121	353.003	8	.000
9	.575	.119	376.147	9	.000
10	.501	.118	394.098	10	.000
11	.423	.117	407.191	11	.000
12	.345	.116	416.096	12	.000
13	.267	.114	421.540	13	.000
14	.189	.113	424.348	14	.000
15	.118	.112	425.469	15	.000
16	.050	.110	425.674	16	.000

The above table shows the autocorrelations for difference lag parameters. The table also has autocorrelation ρ and standard error (SE) for the same along with test statistics i.e. Box-Ljung Test statistic and associated P value. All p values are significant showing that autocorrelations are highly significant. This means that the future prediction or forecasting pretty much depends on present and past values. In other words, the forecasted values highly depend on the historical values of the data series. Figure 1.1 summarizes the results of Table 1.1.

Figure 1.1: Autocorrelations for China FOREX data.

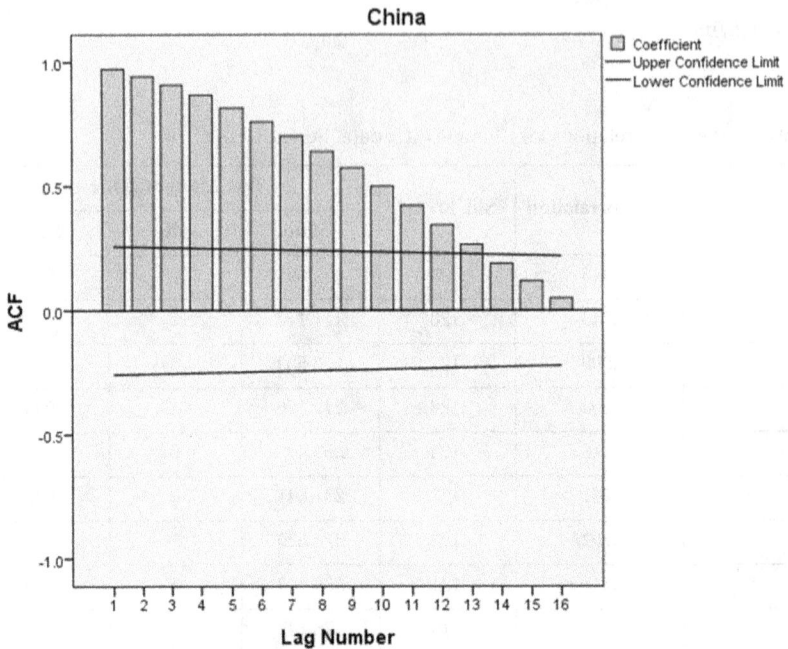

Table 1.2 shows the partial autocorrelations for China's FOREX time series data. A partial correlation does not seem to be that significant as it is clear from Figure 1.2. Moreover, the standard error is observed as the same for all lags. So, it does not matter as what lag justify the good fit. This means, in general, the lag wise differences for partial autocorrelations might not be statistically significant. However, The PACF for the very first lag seems to be significant. The observation does not seem to be true for the rest of the lags.

Table 1.2: Partial Autocorrelations for China FOREX data. Series: China.

Lag	Partial Autocorrelation	Std. Error
1	.973	.132
2	-.076	.132
3	-.080	.132
4	-.142	.132
5	-.210	.132

6	-.072	.132
7	-.075	.132
8	-.048	.132
9	-.076	.132
10	-.177	.132
11	-.110	.132
12	-.046	.132
13	-.027	.132
14	.009	.132
15	.093	.132
16	.005	.132

Figure 1.2: PACF for China's FOREX data.

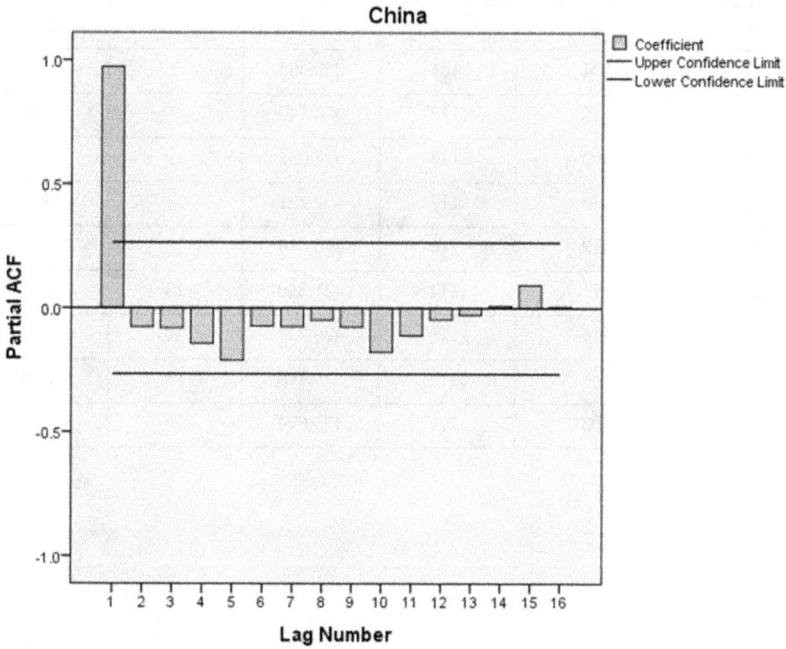

The following section shows the autocorrelations and partial autocorrelations for Indian FOREX data.

1.2. *India*

Table 1.3: Autocorrelations for Indian FOREX data. Series: India.

Lag	Autocorrelation	Std. Error[a]	Box-Ljung Statistic		
			Value	df	Sig.[b]
1	.942	.129	56.849	1	.000
2	.883	.128	111.176	2	.000
3	.826	.127	162.589	3	.000
4	.767	.126	210.356	4	.000
5	.713	.124	253.433	5	.000
6	.672	.123	291.641	6	.000
7	.632	.122	324.829	7	.000
8	.584	.121	353.003	8	.000
9	.545	.119	376.147	9	.000
10	.509	.118	394.098	10	.000
11	.464	.117	407.191	11	.000
12	.419	.116	416.096	12	.000
13	.371	.114	421.540	13	.000
14	.319	.113	424.348	14	.000
15	.261	.112	425.469	15	.000
16	.203	.110	425.674	16	.000

Figure 1.3: Autocorrelations for Indian FOREX data.

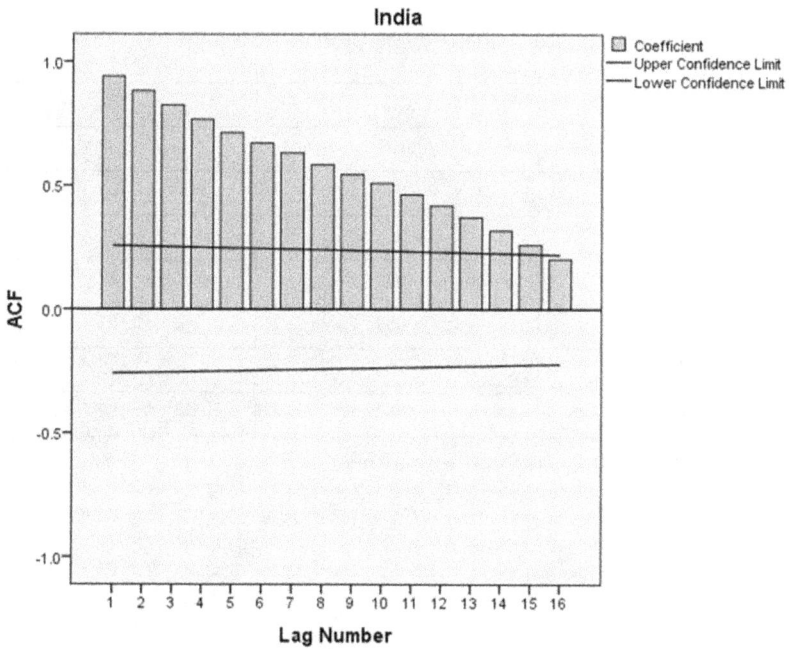

The autocorrelations for Indian FOREX data show that all the correlations are highly significant just like China. From the autocorrelations, it is clear that China seems to be different from India in terms of performance. For India, the autocorrelations are not significant only at lag 16. As such the Indian situation is rather more significant compared to China. This means that the forecasted values highly influenced by present and past data. However, any such observation is premature in the absence of further analysis.

Table 1.4: Partial Autocorrelations for India FOREX data. Series: India.

Lag	Partial Autocorrelation	Std. Error
1	.942	.132
2	-.033	.132
3	-.017	.132
4	-.046	.132
5	.015	.132

6	.073	.132
7	-.009	.132
8	-.094	.132
9	.040	.132
10	.016	.132
11	-.099	.132
12	-.028	.132
13	-.066	.132
14	-.059	.132
15	-.085	.132
16	-.067	.132

Figure 1.4: PACF for Indian FOREX data.

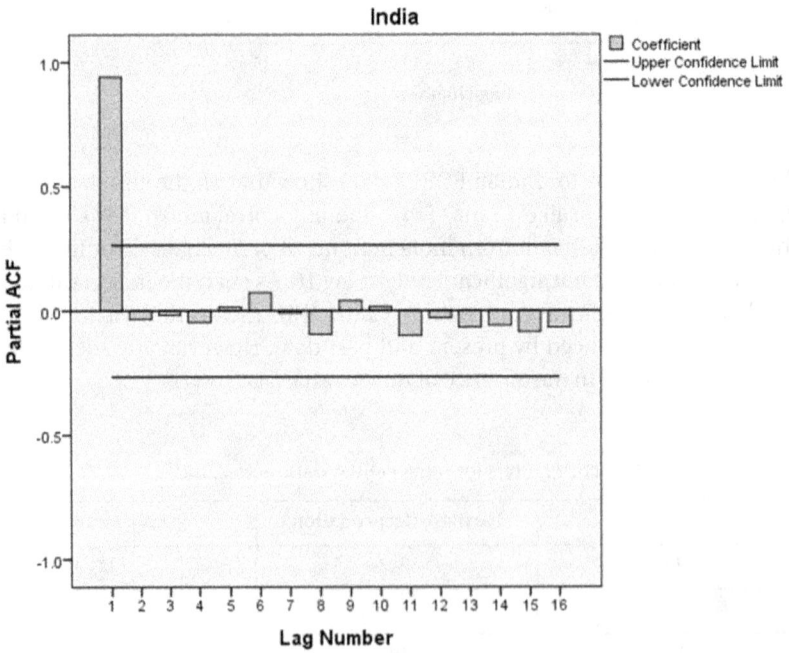

Both Table 1.4 and Figure 1.4 show the status of PACF for Indian FOREX data. The standard error is the same for all lags; this makes it clear that the lag wise differences are not a matter for forecasting. The analysis further shows that there is not any problem of cycles for both the countries, i.e. India and China. The data shows that the cyclical effects are absent. The trend is steady without any random fluctuations which might trigger a cyclical effect on prediction. The very first PACF seems to be significant for Indian FOREX data, but the rest of the lags is pretty much steady. So the cyclical effects are absent. The same is the case for China. So, both countries free from cyclical trends in the forex trade, which is again an interesting observation.

Part 2: Time Series Modeler

This section shows the data analysis for time series analysis and forecasting. This part has three subsections, i.e. model summary and statistics, forecasting and visualization. Table 1.5 shows the model description, and the forecasting is Brown's exponential smoothing. The earlier section Research Methods provide a description of this model.

Table 1.5: Model Description.

			Model Type
Model ID	China	Model_1	Brown
	India	Model_2	Brown

SPSS expert builder predicts or forecasts the data for both countries with the same model i.e. Brown's exponential smoothing model. This again makes it easy to evaluate because the study is a comparative study.

2.1. Model Summary

Table 1.6: Model Fit for China and Indian FOREX data.

Fit Statistic	Stationary R-squared	R-squared	RMSE	MAPE	MaxAPE	MAE	MaxAE	Normalized BIC
Mean	.350	.980	1.174	5.017	26.747	.729	4.390	-.083
SE	.074	.015	1.021	.061	2.329	.686	2.748	2.028
Minimum	.298	.970	.452	4.974	25.100	.244	2.447	-1.517

Maximum		.402	.990	1.896	5.060	28.394	1.214	6.334	1.351
	5	.298	.970	.452	4.974	25.100	.244	2.447	-1.517
	10	.298	.970	.452	4.974	25.100	.244	2.447	-1.517
	25	.298	.970	.452	4.974	25.100	.244	2.447	-1.517
Percentile	50	.350	.980	1.174	5.017	26.747	.729	4.390	-.083
	75	.402	.990	1.896	5.060	28.394	1.214	6.334	1.351
	90	.402	.990	1.896	5.060	28.394	1.214	6.334	1.351
	95	.402	.990	1.896	5.060	28.394	1.214	6.334	1.351

Table 1.6 shows various fit measures (statistics) for the Brown's model on Chinese FOREX data. Perhaps, a more intuitive and useful measure could be the R^2 value which is 0.98 and shows that 98 percent of the regression error is explained by the total error in the data. This shows that the Brown exponential smoothing is highly useful for forecasting. The other values are only useful to recheck the decision whether the model is useful or not. Interestingly the standard error (SE) for R^2 value is also very less (0.015). The rest of the information in the table 1.6 measures for different percentiles of the data. For instance, at 50th percentile the R^2 value appears to be 0.980 and at 95th percentile the R^2 value appears to be 0.990 this shows that the value is monotonously increasing. That shows more support for the model, because the other values of RMSE, MAPE, MAE etc. are also increasing according to the percentile.

Table 1.7: Model Statistics for both Chinese and Indian FOREX data.

Model	Number of Predictors	Model Fit statistics Stationary R-squared	Ljung-Box Q (18)			Number of Outliers
			Statistics	DF	Sig.	
China-Model_1	0	.402	14.320	17	.644	0
India-Model_2	0	.298	17.412	17	.427	0

Table 1.7 shows the Ljung-Box Q Test for Model acceptability. The study evaluated the hypothesis that the data used for analysis is identically independent distributions (IID). P values for both China and India are not significant, so

the study cannot reject the null hypothesis. The stationary R^2 value is not significant. This shows that the error in the data is not that significant.

Table 1.8: Forecasted values for both Chinese and Indian FOREX data.

Model	China-Model_1			India-Model_2		
	Forecast	UCL	LCL	Forecast	UCL	LCL
2017	6.607	7.513	5.702	70.466	74.265	66.667
2018	6.691	8.007	5.375	73.674	79.716	67.633
2019	6.775	8.561	4.989	76.883	85.504	68.261
2020	6.858	9.164	4.552	80.091	91.586	68.596
2021	6.942	9.813	4.071	83.299	97.933	68.665
2022	7.026	10.504	3.548	86.508	104.524	68.492
2023	7.110	11.233	2.986	89.716	111.341	68.091
2024	7.193	11.998	2.389	92.924	118.372	67.477
2025	7.277	12.797	1.757	96.133	125.605	66.661
2026	7.361	13.629	1.092	99.341	133.029	65.653

The analysis estimates for a further 10 years, i.e. till 2026. Table 1.7 shows the forecasted values starting from 2017 to 2026 and shows a steady trend. The very first forecasted value for China is 6.94 this means each US dollar is equal to 6.94 units of Chinese currency, i.e. Yen. The interval estimate for the same appears to be 7.51 and 5.70 which is very close to the estimated or forecasted value for China. The rest of the values are steadily increasing with their respective intervals at 95 percent confidence level. While coming to Indian forecasted results, the very first forecasted value, i.e., for 2017 is 70.46 with confidence interval 74.26 and 66.66. This shows that the Indian currency likely to be traded at 74.26 units of Indian currency.

The forecasting for both the countries is upward and not as volatile as the estimates are closely intact with their confidence intervals. The fitness measures in table 1.7 also show that the model could forecast with a very less error and the values are highly accurate. Moreover, the forecasts show an upward trend, which is similar to the historical data. This gives valid inputs for a decision that the situation is advisable for investments in FOREX trade. Figure 1.5 adds visualization to table 1.7.

Figure 1.5: Actual vs. Forecasted data for China and India.

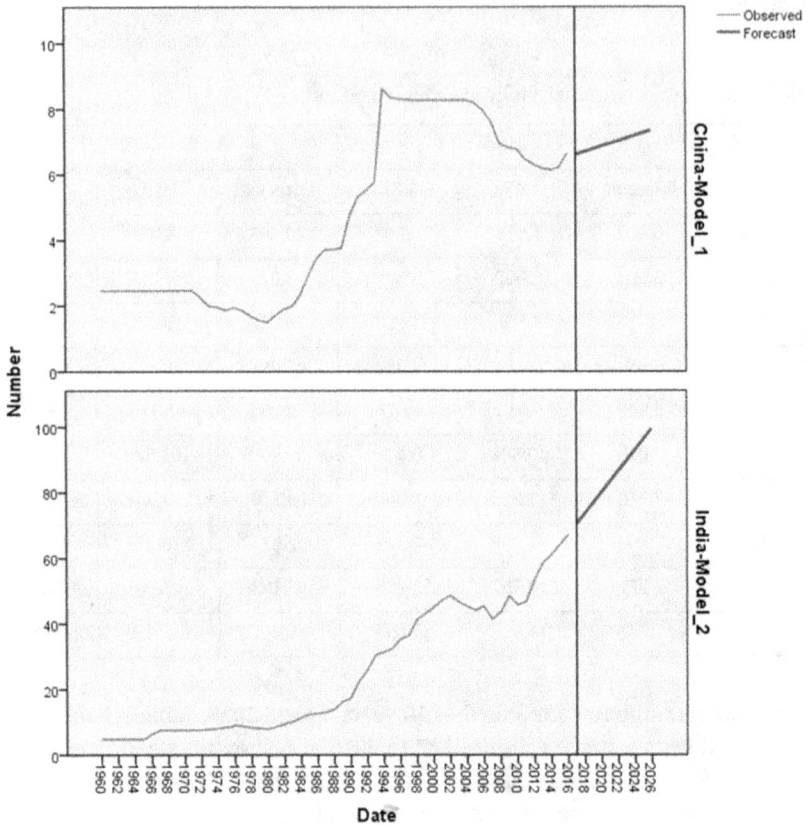

Figure 1.5 throws interesting observations. The Forex trade for China had a dip from 1970 to 1982 and increased after 1982. China struggled in the 1960s due to significant social, political, and economic changes. This might be having an effect over the consecutive years to come in the future, i.e. 1970 to 1980. China suffered from production stagnation, social commotion and turmoil in the rural areas, disruption in transportation. Though the economy improved during early 1970 it suffered in the late 1970s. There were a few reforms which took place during the early 1980s. The early and later times of the 1980s were promising in China, especially the foreign trade enthralled in 1980s.

However, the Indian Forex trade was steadily upward with a minor decrease in the curve after 2002. The Indian political and economic scenario at this time is not so precarious. However, there is little decrease in GDP during this period with increases foreign debt. These two issues might be responsible for the dip in FOREX trade during the early 2000's in India.

Conclusion

The aim of this study is to evaluate Forex trade comparatively with special reference to China and India. The study proposed a hypothesis that the Forex exchange trade performance in these countries is significantly different. The study evaluated forex data for a period of 56 years, i.e. from 1960 to 2016. The future Forex exchange values are forecasted through Brown's exponential smoothing model and the study could not find evidence in support of the hypothesis that the differences are significant. The Brown exponential smoothing model could forecast the future of currency exchange values for a period of 10 years with utmost accuracy. There is an upwards trend in the way currency exchange values are performing between these two countries. The forecasted values are very much following the trend observed in the data. Though the study could not reject the null hypothesis but finds certain interesting cyclical influences which are insignificant. The historical study shows that the currency exchange is highly influenced by the political, social and cultural changes in China. However, there is no such influence over Indian currency exchange prices.

References

Fratzscher, M., Mehl., A. (2011). China's Dominance Hypothesis and the Emergence of a Tri-Polar Global Currency System. Working Paper Series, No 1392 / October 2011. This paper can be downloaded without charge from http://www.ecb.europa.eu or from the Social Science Research Network electronic library at http://ssrn.com/abstract_id=1935891.

Ito, H., et al. (2008) Emerging market currency composition of reserves, denomination of trade and currency movements. http://web.pdx.edu/~ito/Ito%20McCauley%20Chan%20paper.pdf

McCauley, R and Scatigna, M (2011). Foreign exchange trading in emerging currencies: more financial, more offshore. BIS Quarterly Review, 67 – 75.

Patnaik, I., and Shah, A. (2009). The difficulties of the Chinese and Indian exchange rate regimes. The European Journal of Comparative Economics Vol. 6, n.1, pp. 157-173 ISSN 1722-4667.

Suresh, A., (2012). Exchange Rate Impact on Bilateral Trade between India and China. Journal of Finance, Accounting and Management, 3(2), 15-41.

Chapter 2

India's Exchange Traded Currency Derivatives Market: An Overview

Gangineni Dhananjhay,
Professor (Finance), MBA Department,
Narayana Engineering College, Nellore (A.P), 524004.
Mobile No.: 09391319721
Email: gdhananjhay@gmail.com

Prof. S. S. Prasada Rao,
Dean, Academic Affairs,
GITAM University, Visakhapatnam.
Email: profsspr@gmail.com

Introduction

"Changes in the international financial structure will create a great expansion in the demand for foreign cover. It is highly desirable that this demand be met by as broad, as deep, as resilient a futures market in foreign currencies as possible in order to facilitate foreign trade and investment." - Prof. Milton Friedman

Globally foreign exchange (FX) is the largest liquid market. The cash value traded exceeds USD 4 trillion/day. Currency markets are 24-hour markets in the true sense. The launch of currency futures market has been a major landmark in the global financial market's history. The Chicago Mercantile Exchange (CME) became the first currency futures exchange. In India, NSE was the first exchange to launch currency derivatives segment on August 29, 2008, followed by BSE on October 1, 2008, and MCX's affiliate MCX-SX on Oct 9, 2008, and finally USE on September 2010. In India, currency derivatives had a modest beginning but gained credibility and acceptability. Currency Derivatives (CD) market has completed five years of successful operation in India. The CD segment has witnessed a rapid development, aided by market microstructural factors like lower transaction costs and intense competition by exchanges offering the same product.

Background

The currency market is interlinked with all other financial markets. The linkages are so strong that it is probably outdated to speak of the stock market, FX market, bond market and the commodities market as though there is a watertight separation between them. The Chicago Mercantile Exchange (CME) created FX futures, the first ever financial futures contracts in 1972. The contracts were created under the guidance of Leo Me lamed, the CME chairman. The Forex contract capitalized on the U.S abandonment of the Bretton Woods agreement, which had fixed world exchange rates to a gold standard after World War 2. The abandonment of the Bretton Woods agreement resulted in currency values being allowed to float, increasing business risk. CME currency futures extended the reach of risk management beyond commodities, which were the main derivative contracts traded at CME until then. The concept of currency futures at CME was revolutionary and gained credibility through the endorsement of Nobel-prize winning economist Milton Friedman.

Currency Derivatives Trading Mechanism

NSE's currency derivatives segment provides trading in derivative instruments like currency futures on 4 currency pairs, currency options on US Dollars and Interest rate futures on 10Y GS and 91D T-Bill. The NSE trading system called National Exchange for Automated Trading (NEAT) is a fully automated screen-based trading system, which follows the principle of an order driven market.

Currency Pairs available for futures trading:

USDINR – Futures and Options   (US Dollar, Indian Rupee)

EURINR- Futures   (European Euro, Indian Rupee)

GBPINR – Futures   (British Pound, Indian Rupee)

JPYINR - Futures   (Japanese Yen, Indian Rupee)

Literature Review

We have reviewed some recently published literature pertaining to India's exchange traded currency derivatives markets.

Chowdary (2012) discusses the concerns in the futures market. As evident from the existing literature, currency derivatives can be used for hedging Forex risks, speculation or arbitrage. He further concludes that equity was gloomy and commodity was dull whereas the entire glitter is in the currency market.

Mathur (2012) states that currency trading accounts for more than 60 percent of global trading and marks as one of the world's largest financial markets in the world followed by commodities and equities. The researcher indicates that the world is shifting from non-transparent OTC products to Exchange Traded products.

Srinivasan (2012) emphasizes that near-explosive growth of the FX futures market in India. The paper notes that the trend is now to move as much of the OTC trading activity as possible to the exchange traded and centrally cleared markets. The researcher opines that growth in the Indian FX futures market is not really surprising given the wide-spread interest in FX.

SEBI (2010) states that the turnover in 'currency futures', both in absolute terms as well as a percentage of OTC currency forward turnover has been increasing, ever since the start of currency futures trading. The study further concludes that the currency futures market has been operating at a bid-ask spread which is narrower than that of the OTC currency spot market. It notes that the futures and the forward rate diverged at the beginning of trading in the currency futures market over-time, the rates have appeared to converge reflecting gradual disappearance of arbitrage opportunity between the two markets.

Upadhyay (2009) finds that the regulations that apply to the currency futures market in India. He also examines the applications of currency futures and studies the performance of USD-INR futures contract since inception at NSE. The researcher notes the robust growth of futures contracts since their launch. The study recommends that the RBI should allow the FIIs and NRIs to participate in the currency derivative markets in a phased manner.

Sarang (2012) report finds the reasons behind the introduction of currency futures and its growth trajectory. The report further analyses the participation of currency futures in the volatility of the trading system.

Growth of Indian Currency Derivatives Market

Trends in Currency Derivatives Segment

In 2016-17 the aggregate turnover in the currency derivatives segment at the exchanges increased by 4.3 percent to Rs. 69, 62,833 crore from Rs. 66, 76,821 crore in 2015-16. During 2016-17, the total turnover was the highest at NSE (48, 57,076 crore), followed by BSE (18, 07,829 crore) and MSEI (2, 97,928 crore). NSE accounted for 69.8 percent of the total turnover in the currency segment followed by BSE (26.0 percent) and MSEI (4.3 percent). Globally, currency derivatives' volumes have increased significantly since 2005, with a 10.4 percent increase in volumes traded in 2016 over the previous calendar year. The volumes were up for both options and futures with an increase of 39.3 and 4.0 percent respectively in 2016. As per the WFE's 2016 report, NSE was the second exchange in the world in currency derivatives in terms of the number of contracts traded in both futures and options segments. Moreover, as per the report, the increase in volume traded in the Asia-Pacific region in 2016 was mainly driven by an increase in volumes at BSE (23 percent) and NSE (22 percent).

Trends in the Currency Derivatives Segment

Table 2.1: Trading Statistics of Currency Derivatives Segment.

Month	NSE		MSEI		USE		BSE	
	Traded Value (crore)	Open interest at the end of Value (crore)	Traded Value (crore)	Open interest at the end of Traded Value (crore)	Traded Value (crore)	Open interest at the end of Value (crore)	Traded Value (crore)	Open interest at the end of Value (crore)
1	3	5	7	9	11	13	15	17
Apr-10	3,45,932	2,679	3,73,372	2,522	Na	Na	Na	Na
May-10	3,59,680	3,702	4,23,075	2,644	Na	Na	Na	Na
Jun-10	3,27,382	4,600	4,25,088	3,929	Na	Na	Na	Na
Jul-10	2,13,353	4,057	3,20,016	3,693	Na	Na	Na	Na
Aug-10	2,01,239	4,514	2,91,018	3,808	Na	Na	Na	Na
Sep-10	2,84,704	3,876	3,66,195	4,115	2,17,627	606	Na	Na
Oct-10	3,05,597	4,645	3,58,429	3,679	2,41,810	240	Na	Na
Nov-10	2,66,332	6,828	3,32,253	4,246	78,399	459	Na	Na
Dec-10	2,37,564	6,540	2,76,019	3,736	29,961	309	Na	Na
Jan-11	2,74,833	9,000	3,41,913	4,146	43,330	148	Na	Na
Feb-11	2,54,654	10,540	2,82,742	3,567	60,569	92	Na	Na
Mar-11	3,78,517	13,690	4,03,898	3,706	90,806	109	Na	Na
Apr-11	3,48,467	14,673	2,70,381	3,844	1,03,427	219	Na	Na
May-11	4,32,502	15,437	3,57,484	3,519	2,10,512	251	Na	Na
Jun-11	4,42,877	19,505	3,67,456	5,075	2,28,677	886	Na	Na

Jul-11	5,55,282	27,081	4,08,314	7,218	2,82,514	1,504	Na	Na
Aug-11	5,85,123	20,465	4,50,762	5,943	3,29,582	1,083	Na	Na
Sep-11	4,11,553	18,213	3,71,558	4,836	1,94,820	666	Na	Na
Oct-11	2,73,114	18,247	2,33,541	5,484	71,145	529	Na	Na
Nov-11	3,21,666	19,339	2,75,674	6,326	38,840	313	Na	Na
Dec-11	3,31,805	12,886	2,64,005	5,269	12,580	168	Na	Na
Jan-12	3,59,481	15,513	2,45,250	5,132	6,609	104	Na	Na
Feb-12	2,96,896	15,149	2,15,374	5,269	5,652	114	Na	Na
Mar-12	3,16,224	15,328	2,72,645	4,494	7,423	125	Na	Na
Apr-12	2,60,451	17,737	1,97,708	8,872	805	84	Na	Na
May-12	4,53,946	19,913	3,37,677	7,777	1,193	52	Na	Na
Jun-12	3,93,619	19,918	2,71,484	7,788	1,191	61	Na	Na
Jul-12	4,67,274	18,388	2,97,670	6,754	1,768	56	Na	Na
Aug-12	3,28,907	18,694	2,09,916	7,373	1,290	44	Na	Na
Sep-12	3,97,592	18,451	2,52,627	6,121	1,888	17	Na	Na
Oct-12	5,07,426	18,825	2,91,772	7,091	2,950	40	Na	Na
Nov-12	4,67,875	25,176	2,62,790	7,989	2,639	50	Na	Na
Dec-12	4,48,753	22,872	2,42,176	7,861	18,385	64	Na	Na
Jan-13	5,86,025	25,155	3,33,353	7,647	26,722	73	Na	Na
Feb-13	4,97,277	26,399	2,87,002	8,107	27,374	319	Na	Na
Mar-13	4,65,320	20,101	3,19,004	7,389	46,657	292	Na	Na
Apr-13	4,41,682	25,188	2,84,076	9,284	17,033	53	Na	Na
May-13	5,78,460	30,349	3,82,441	11,431	24,074	81	Na	Na
Jun-13	7,75,313	28,247	4,82,880	9,989	22,587	69	Na	Na
Jul-13	4,09,739	11,360	3,10,899	8,263	21,896	84	Na	Na
Aug-13	3,40,807	10,494	2,33,007	3,886	22,989	162	Na	Na
Sep-13	3,03,632	7,568	1,78,614	2,619	19,791	147	Na	Na
Oct-13	2,21,371	6,866	1,18,610	2,349	21,242	106	Na	Na
Nov-13	1,97,909	7,537	88,360	2,340	16,757	74	325	1
Dec-13	1,86,064	7,493	87,641	2,624	19,016	142	17,227	133

Jan-14	2,08,564	7,385	1,00,374	2,646	21,669	140	42,396	212
Feb-14	1,61,726	6,780	72,031	2,772	24,440	200	74,944	387
Mar-14	1,87,245	6,409	83,477	2,156	70,126	217	1,09,420	253
Apr-14	1,55,082	7,867	59,277	2,575	2,940	163	71,908	458
May-14	2,14,584	9,468	80,014	3,184	5,413	243	1,13,141	1,228
Jun-14	2,08,376	13,499	68,288	4,685	5,005	242	1,03,749	1,477
Jul-14	2,49,632	18,529	78,692	5,602	6,244	263	1,17,526	1,947
Aug-14	2,61,636	17,882	62,995	4,516	8,202	255	1,15,127	2,641
Sep-14	2,85,236	17,728	57,590	3,577	9,370	179	1,41,170	2,690
Oct-14	2,29,235	20,103	41,661	4,326	6,146	116	1,07,439	4,216
Nov-14	2,02,966	25,746	36,889	4,926	6,573	91	1,16,741	5,094
Dec-14	2,94,820	20,324	48,923	2,743	2,292	58	1,87,115	3,195
Jan-15	3,60,256	17,898	43,489	3,055	Na	Na	3,17,692	4,465
Feb-15	2,25,058	20,722	29,927	3,267	Na	Na	2,25,366	5,436
Mar-15	3,37,027	20,793	42,181	2,292	Na	Na	2,91,569	4,161
Apr-15	2,98,618	21,788	37,928	2,783	Na	Na	2,25,797	5,813
May-15	3,19,780	19,525	35,710	2,327	Na	Na	2,41,997	4,939
Jun-15	3,12,262	20,127	37,180	3,758	Na	Na	2,12,632	7,099
Jul-15	2,82,764	13,691	29,813	3,652	Na	Na	2,12,065	6,060
Aug-15	4,47,028	11,642	35,783	2,019	Na	Na	2,70,931	4,767
Sep-15	3,72,159	10,482	28,926	1,455	Na	Na	1,97,052	4,172
Oct-15	3,57,978	10,771	22,351	2,383	Na	Na	1,86,708	4,730
Nov-15	3,35,711	21,700	19,275	1,728	Na	Na	1,80,138	5,244
Dec-15	3,55,065	28,554	15,817	1,968	Na	Na	1,93,962	7,493
Jan-16	4,84,843	26,399	19,734	1,566	Na	Na	2,91,773	6,653
Feb-16	4,59,009	29,708	19,944	1,828	Na	Na	2,74,638	8,163
Mar-16	4,76,669	29,814	22,114	2,162	Na	Na	2,76,236	8,554
Apr-16	3,48,331	27,563	17,805	1,873	Na	Na	2,70,391	7,895
May-16	4,26,597	27,556	25,581	1,551	Na	Na	3,21,421	6,952
Jun-16	5,47,668	26,709	43,440	1,395	Na	Na	3,53,598	6,944

Jul-16	3,15,239	26,891	29,763	1,822	Na	Na	2,27,277	8,279
Aug-16	3,36,005	33,133	27,177	2,009	Na	Na	2,36,833	9,260
Sep-16	4,23,296	35,044	33,924	2,014	Na	Na	2,61,357	9,841
Oct-16	3,03,829	28,856	24,370	1,721	Na	Na	2,08,961	9,691
Nov-16	5,54,009	32,050	33,466	1,826	Na	Na	3,02,327	10,740
Dec-16	4,38,729	29,903	19,999	1,347	Na	Na	2,56,606	8,099
Average	**3,53,472**	**17,485**	**1,83,729**	**4,263**	**52,711**	**234**	**1,90,212**	**4,984**
Standard deviation	**1,17,498**	**8,383**	**1,44,378**	**2,344**	**81,283**	**277**	**88,958**	**3,117**

Notes: 1. Currency Futures trading started at USE on September 20th, 2010.
       2. Currency Options were introduced at NSE and USE w.e.f October 29th, 2010.
       3. Trading in currency derivatives at BSE started since November'13.
       4. USE has stopped providing trading facilities from December 30, 2014.
Source: NSE, MSEI, USE and BSE.

Table 2.2: Instrument Wise Turnover and Open Interest in Currency Derivatives Segment of BSE (in percent).

Month	Turnover				Open Interest as on last day of the month (in lots)			
	USDINR	EURINR	GBPINR	JPYINR	USDINR	EURINR	GBPINR	GBPINR
Nov-13	100.0	0.0	0.0	0.0	100.0	0.0	0.0	0.0
Dec-13	99.2	0.5	0.2	0.1	69.5	27.8	2.8	0.0
Jan-14	99.3	0.4	0.3	0.1	76.3	23.1	0.6	0.0
Feb-14	99.0	0.3	0.2	0.5	85.3	6.6	6.0	2.2
Mar-14	97.3	1.1	1.4	0.2	96.6	2.9	0.5	0.0
Apr-14	99.3	0.3	0.4	0.0	96.9	0.9	2.3	0.0
May-14	99.5	0.3	0.3	0.0	94.7	2.7	2.6	0.0
Jun-14	99.5	0.2	0.2	0.1	95.6	2.3	2.1	0.0
Jul-14	99.4	0.1	0.1	0.4	96.7	1.7	1.6	0.0
Aug-14	99.7	0.0	0.1	0.2	99.8	0.1	0.0	0.0
Sep-14	99.5	0.0	0.1	0.5	99.9	0.0	0.0	0.0
Oct-14	99.1	0.3	0.3	0.3	99.7	0.0	0.1	0.2
Nov-14	99.5	0.0	0.1	0.4	100.0	0.0	0.0	0.0
Dec-14	99.6	0.0	0.1	0.3	100.0	0.0	0.0	0.0

Jan-15	99.7	0.0	0.1	0.1	99.7	0.2	0.2	0.0
Feb-15	99.8	0.0	0.1	0.1	99.9	0.0	0.1	0.1
Mar-15	99.5	0.5	0.0	0.0	99.8	0.1	0.1	0.1
Apr-15	99.6	0.3	0.1	0.0	99.9	0.1	0.0	0.1
May-15	99.7	0.2	0.1	0.0	99.9	0.1	0.1	0.1
Jun-15	99.6	0.2	0.1	0.0	99.6	0.1	0.2	0.1
Jul-15	99.7	0.2	0.1	0.0	99.9	0.1	0.1	0.1
Aug-15	99.8	0.1	0.1	0.0	99.6	0.2	0.1	0.1
Sep-15	99.6	0.2	0.1	0.1	99.7	0.2	0.2	0.1
Oct-15	99.6	0.1	0.2	0.0	99.8	0.1	0.1	0.1
Nov-15	99.4	0.4	0.1	0.0	99.7	0.1	0.2	0.0
Dec-15	99.7	0.1	0.2	0.0	99.8	0.1	0.1	0.0
Jan-16	99.5	0.4	0.1	0.1	99.6	0.3	0.0	0.1
Feb-16	99.4	0.4	0.1	0.1	99.8	0.1	0.1	0.0
Mar-16	99.3	0.6	0.1	0.0	99.1	0.9	0.1	0.0
Apr-16	99.5	0.4	0.1	0.0	99.5	0.2	0.1	0.1
May-16	99.3	0.4	0.2	0.1	99.2	0.5	0.3	0.0
Jun-16	99.1	0.4	0.4	0.1	99.3	0.4	0.3	0.1
Jul-16	99.0	0.3	0.5	0.2	99.6	0.2	0.2	0.1
Aug-16	99.1	0.3	0.4	0.2	99.5	0.2	0.2	0.1
Sep-16	99.1	0.3	0.4	0.3	98.8	0.3	0.6	0.3
Oct-16	99.0	0.2	0.6	0.2	99.6	0.1	0.1	0.2
Nov-16	99.4	0.3	0.2	0.2	99.7	0.1	0.1	0.1
Dec-16	99.6	0.2	0.1	0.1	99.8	0.1	0.0	0.1
Average	**99.4**	**0.3**	**0.2**	**0.1**	**97.4**	**1.9**	**0.6**	**0.1**
Standard deviation	0.4	0.2	0.2	0.1	6.5	5.8	1.2	0.4

Note: Trading in currency derivatives at BSE started since November'13.
Source: BSE.

Table 2.3: Instrument Wise Turnover and Open Interest in Currency Derivatives Segment of NSE (in percent).

Month	Turnover				Open Interest as on last day of the month (in lots)			
	USDINR	EURINR	GBPINR	JPYINR	USDINR	EURINR	GBPINR	JPYINR
Apr-10	97.1	2.8	0.1	0.0	95.3	3.7	1.0	0.1
May-10	95.6	4.2	0.2	0.0	96.7	2.6	0.5	0.2
Jun-10	97.4	2.4	0.2	0.1	96.6	2.0	0.8	0.6
Jul-10	95.1	4.3	0.4	0.2	96.3	2.6	0.7	0.4
Aug-10	95.9	3.6	0.3	0.2	96.2	2.2	0.4	1.1
Sep-10	97.8	1.6	0.3	0.4	95.0	2.8	0.5	1.7
Oct-10	97.6	1.6	0.4	0.5	94.7	2.4	0.5	2.4
Nov-10	96.3	2.2	0.8	0.6	95.9	1.8	0.7	1.7
Dec-10	96.4	2.1	0.7	0.8	96.0	1.4	0.9	1.8
Jan-11	95.5	3.0	0.9	0.6	95.1	2.9	0.7	1.4
Feb-11	96.1	2.3	0.9	0.7	95.8	2.3	0.8	1.1
Mar-11	95.5	2.4	0.9	1.2	96.8	2.4	0.3	0.5
Apr-11	96.5	2.5	0.6	0.4	96.6	2.6	0.5	0.3
May-11	95.6	3.1	0.8	0.5	97.3	1.8	0.5	0.5
Jun-11	94.8	3.3	1.3	0.6	97.5	1.6	0.5	0.4
Jul-11	94.5	3.6	1.3	0.6	97.8	0.9	0.2	1.1
Aug-11	95.0	3.0	1.0	1.1	96.1	1.8	0.6	1.4
Sep-11	97.2	1.6	0.6	0.7	98.1	0.9	0.3	0.7
Oct-11	97.3	1.6	0.5	0.6	98.2	1.3	0.2	0.3
Nov-11	97.5	1.4	0.6	0.4	98.2	1.2	0.3	0.3
Dec-11	97.7	1.1	0.7	0.5	97.7	1.5	0.3	0.5
Jan-12	98.3	0.9	0.5	0.3	98.6	0.7	0.2	0.5
Feb-12	98.4	0.8	0.5	0.3	98.0	1.0	0.5	0.4
Mar-12	98.3	0.8	0.5	0.4	98.1	1.0	0.6	0.3
Apr-12	98.2	0.8	0.5	0.4	98.2	1.1	0.4	0.3
May-12	98.7	0.6	0.4	0.3	98.6	0.8	0.4	0.3

Jun-12	98.6	0.6	0.4	0.4	98.4	0.9	0.4	0.3
Jul-12	98.8	0.6	0.3	0.3	98.5	0.6	0.5	0.3
Aug-12	98.4	0.6	0.6	0.4	98.0	0.9	0.8	0.3
Sep-12	98.1	1.0	0.5	0.4	98.4	0.8	0.5	0.2
Oct-12	98.4	0.8	0.4	0.3	97.3	1.7	0.7	0.3
Nov-12	98.2	0.9	0.5	0.4	98.0	1.2	0.6	0.2
Dec-12	97.2	1.5	0.6	0.6	97.2	1.8	0.7	0.2
Jan-13	96.8	1.8	0.6	0.9	97.5	1.7	0.3	0.5
Feb-13	95.8	2.2	1.0	1.1	98.2	1.2	0.3	0.3
Mar-13	96.2	1.8	1.0	1.0	98.0	1.2	0.3	0.4
Apr-13	95.5	1.7	1.0	1.7	97.8	1.3	0.4	0.5
May-13	96.1	1.7	1.1	1.1	97.3	1.7	0.6	0.4
Jun-13	97.0	1.3	0.9	0.7	97.1	1.8	0.7	0.3
Jul-13	93.8	3.2	2.1	0.9	91.7	5.3	2.4	0.6
Aug-13	88.2	5.6	4.5	1.6	93.9	4.0	1.8	0.4
Sep-13	88.1	5.0	5.3	1.6	92.3	4.9	2.1	0.7
Oct-13	90.5	4.4	3.6	1.4	92.3	4.9	2.1	0.7
Nov-13	90.1	4.6	4.1	1.3	91.9	4.4	3.0	0.7
Dec-13	87.5	5.4	5.6	1.5	91.5	4.5	3.2	0.8
Jan-14	87.2	5.1	6.3	1.5	91.8	4.2	3.4	0.6
Feb-14	87.0	5.3	6.3	1.5	90.4	5.4	3.7	0.4
Mar-14	88.6	4.9	5.4	1.2	93.3	4.1	1.9	0.7
Apr-14	89.1	4.9	4.7	1.3	92.2	4.7	2.5	0.7
May-14	88.9	4.8	5.2	1.1	90.3	5.1	4.0	0.7
Jun-14	88.6	5.1	5.3	1.0	94.2	3.1	2.4	0.4
Jul-14	91.4	3.5	4.3	0.7	96.0	2.0	1.7	0.3
Aug-14	94.1	2.2	3.2	0.5	96.7	1.6	1.4	0.3
Sep-14	93.3	2.5	3.6	0.7	96.7	1.5	1.5	0.3
Oct-14	92.7	3.2	3.2	0.9	96.7	1.6	1.1	0.6
Nov-14	90.9	3.6	3.9	1.5	97.1	1.5	1.0	0.4

Dec-14	92.5	3.0	3.4	1.2	97.3	1.4	0.9	0.4
Jan-15	92.6	3.1	3.1	1.2	97.6	1.6	0.8	0.5
Feb-15	91.4	3.2	4.1	1.3	97.3	1.3	1.4	0.4
Mar-15	92.4	3.3	3.4	0.9	97.4	1.6	1.1	0.3
Apr-15	92.1	3.6	3.6	0.7	96.4	2.0	1.5	0.3
May-15	92.4	3.3	3.6	0.7	96.7	1.9	1.4	0.5
Jun-15	91.4	4.2	3.4	0.9	97.3	1.5	1.2	0.2
Jul-15	90.8	4.4	4.1	0.8	97.2	1.5	1.4	0.3
Aug-15	94.0	2.8	2.6	0.6	96.8	1.9	1.3	0.3
Sep-15	93.1	3.2	3.0	0.7	97.1	1.6	1.3	0.4
Oct-15	94.0	2.8	2.7	0.5	97.6	1.3	1.1	0.4
Nov-15	95.0	2.3	2.3	0.4	97.6	1.3	1.1	0.2
Dec-15	93.5	2.9	3.1	0.5	97.6	1.3	1.1	0.2
Jan-16	94.8	2.3	2.3	0.7	97.6	1.5	0.6	0.3
Feb-16	93.4	2.9	2.6	1.1	97.6	1.3	0.6	0.5
Mar-16	94.5	2.5	2.5	0.6	97.8	1.5	0.5	0.2
Apr-16	93.7	2.2	3.2	0.9	97.0	1.3	0.9	0.7
May-16	92.8	2.1	4.0	1.1	96.8	1.6	1.2	0.4
Jun-16	89.8	2.1	6.6	1.5	96.5	1.2	1.1	1.2
Jul-16	89.0	2.6	6.1	2.3	96.1	1.7	1.1	1.1
Aug-16	91.2	2.5	4.2	2.1	96.8	1.6	0.7	0.9
Sep-16	92.6	2.1	3.2	2.1	96.4	1.1	1.4	1.0
Oct-16	91.8	2.1	4.7	1.5	96.9	1.0	1.5	0.6
Nov-16	94.8	1.6	2.3	1.3	98.0	0.9	0.6	0.5
Dec-16	95.7	1.6	1.9	0.8	97.6	1.0	0.6	0.8
Average	**94.2**	**2.7**	**2.3**	**0.8**	**96.4**	**2.0**	**1.1**	**0.6**
Standard deviation	**3.26**	**1.32**	**1.86**	**0.50**	**2.02**	**1.21**	**0.83**	**0.41**

Source: NSE.

Table 2.4: Instrument Wise Turnover and Open Interest in Currency Derivatives Segment of MSEI (in percent).

Month	Turnover				Open Interest as on last day of the month(in lots)			
	USDINR	EURINR	GBPINR	JPYINR	USDINR	EURINR	GBPINR	JPYINR
Apr-10	89.8	7.1	2.2	0.9	93.8	3.0	2.1	1.0
May-10	87.5	9.5	2.0	1.0	93.5	3.5	1.9	1.0
Jun-10	87.2	10.5	1.5	0.8	96.0	2.1	1.2	0.7
Jul-10	88.7	9.0	1.5	0.9	95.6	2.0	1.1	1.2
Aug-10	91.1	7.5	1.0	0.4	94.6	2.3	0.8	2.3
Sep-10	96.2	2.4	0.7	0.7	96.9	1.6	0.5	1.1
Oct-10	98.3	1.0	0.4	0.2	96.1	1.7	0.7	1.5
Nov-10	97.4	1.7	0.6	0.3	96.5	2.2	0.5	0.8
Dec-10	96.7	2.3	0.7	0.3	94.8	2.2	1.8	1.3
Jan-11	95.1	3.6	1.0	0.3	91.2	5.0	2.1	1.8
Feb-11	95.3	3.1	1.0	0.5	91.2	4.4	2.2	2.2
Mar-11	94.6	3.2	1.0	1.2	90.1	6.6	1.5	1.8
Apr-11	93.9	4.3	1.1	0.6	87.0	11.1	1.1	0.8
May-11	92.9	5.4	1.1	0.6	83.7	10.7	4.2	1.4
Jun-11	90.3	6.6	2.3	0.8	87.0	7.1	4.6	1.2
Jul-11	88.2	8.5	2.3	1.0	91.7	3.3	1.2	3.8
Aug-11	90.4	6.5	1.6	1.6	87.0	6.2	2.5	4.3
Sep-11	93.8	4.3	0.9	1.0	93.9	2.6	1.3	2.2
Oct-11	94.7	3.3	1.0	0.9	93.3	3.6	1.5	1.7
Nov-11	95.8	2.4	1.0	0.8	94.8	2.2	1.5	1.5
Dec-11	96.1	2.2	1.2	0.5	94.2	2.2	2.1	1.5
Jan-12	95.8	2.6	1.0	0.6	95.5	1.9	1.1	1.6
Feb-12	95.9	2.6	0.9	0.6	93.9	2.4	2.2	1.6
Mar-12	95.6	2.3	1.2	1.0	91.7	4.0	3.6	0.8
Apr-12	94.9	2.6	1.5	1.0	96.0	1.6	1.9	0.5
May-12	96.1	2.1	1.2	0.6	94.8	2.1	1.9	1.2

Jun-12	95.5	2.3	1.3	0.9	96.1	1.6	1.4	0.8
Jul-12	95.9	2.0	1.0	1.1	95.2	1.9	1.7	1.2
Aug-12	95.8	1.7	1.3	1.3	95.3	1.7	1.7	1.2
Sep-12	95.4	2.1	1.4	1.2	95.8	2.0	1.1	1.2
Oct-12	95.7	2.0	1.0	1.2	95.3	2.3	1.5	1.0
Nov-12	94.7	2.6	1.4	1.3	94.8	2.8	1.6	0.8
Dec-12	93.6	3.3	1.7	1.4	93.2	4.1	1.9	0.8
Jan-13	93.6	3.1	1.4	1.8	93.6	3.8	0.7	1.9
Feb-13	92.1	3.6	2.0	2.3	95.9	2.5	0.7	0.9
Mar-13	94.2	2.6	1.5	1.7	96.9	1.5	0.7	0.9
Apr-13	93.5	2.4	1.4	2.6	96.1	2.0	0.8	1.1
May-13	93.9	2.5	1.7	1.8	95.1	3.2	1.1	0.6
Jun-13	94.2	2.4	1.8	1.5	93.8	3.7	1.7	0.8
Jul-13	91.6	4.1	3.0	1.3	92.2	4.9	2.3	0.6
Aug-13	86.6	6.1	5.2	2.1	92.7	4.2	2.6	0.5
Sep-13	87.2	5.3	5.5	2.1	93.4	3.9	2.1	0.6
Oct-13	86.7	5.9	5.5	1.9	91.0	5.2	2.6	1.3
Nov-13	86.8	5.6	6.0	1.7	92.4	3.5	3.3	0.8
Dec-13	84.8	6.7	6.6	1.9	91.0	3.5	4.2	1.2
Jan-14	83.6	6.2	8.1	2.0	90.0	4.8	4.6	0.6
Feb-14	82.4	6.8	8.5	2.3	90.6	4.5	4.2	0.7
Mar-14	85.5	5.5	7.1	2.0	91.7	4.2	3.2	0.9
Apr-14	85.3	5.8	6.9	2.1	94.2	2.4	2.9	0.5
May-14	87.1	4.8	6.7	1.4	90.2	4.5	4.5	0.7
Jun-14	87.3	4.8	6.6	1.3	94.7	2.2	2.6	0.5
Jul-14	90.2	3.7	5.0	1.1	95.4	2.3	2.0	0.3
Aug-14	91.0	2.9	5.1	0.9	96.7	1.6	1.5	0.2
Sep-14	89.2	3.2	6.3	1.2	96.3	1.3	2.2	0.3
Oct-14	89.4	3.6	5.6	1.4	97.0	1.3	1.2	0.5
Nov-14	88.2	3.9	5.8	2.0	97.0	1.3	1.1	0.6

Dec-14	90.8	2.7	5.1	1.4	97.9	0.8	0.9	0.4
Jan-15	88.6	4.1	5.5	1.7	97.7	1.3	1.0	0.4
Feb-15	89.1	3.3	6.1	1.5	98.6	0.7	0.7	0.4
Mar-15	89.5	3.9	5.5	1.2	97.1	1.6	1.2	0.1
Apr-15	91.7	3.6	4.1	0.6	97.7	1.4	0.9	0.1
May-15	92.5	3.4	3.6	0.5	96.9	2.4	0.7	0.7
Jun-15	92.6	4.0	2.9	0.5	97.2	2.1	0.7	0.1
Jul-15	87.6	6.6	5.3	0.5	97.0	2.3	0.8	0.1
Aug-15	91.5	4.3	3.8	0.4	97.0	2.1	1.0	0.0
Sep-15	91.8	4.0	3.6	0.6	97.8	1.3	0.9	0.2
Oct-15	91.0	4.4	4.0	0.6	98.4	1.0	0.6	0.1
Nov-15	94.6	2.1	3.0	0.3	98.4	0.9	0.7	0.0
Dec-15	90.1	5.2	4.1	0.5	97.4	1.7	0.9	0.2
Jan-16	91.0	4.4	3.6	1.0	97.0	2.0	0.6	0.3
Feb-16	89.4	4.9	4.6	1.2	96.8	1.2	1.7	0.3
Mar-16	92.6	2.9	4.1	0.4	97.8	1.0	1.0	0.2
Apr-16	94.2	1.6	3.5	0.7	96.8	1.3	1.0	0.9
May-16	95.6	1.4	2.6	0.5	97.0	1.9	0.7	0.4
Jun-16	96.7	0.9	1.9	0.5	97.1	0.7	0.8	1.4
Jul-16	97.0	0.7	1.5	0.8	98.1	0.6	0.6	0.7
Aug-16	97.1	0.9	1.2	0.8	97.9	0.8	0.5	0.9
Sep-16	97.9	0.5	0.9	0.8	98.2	0.2	0.7	0.9
Oct-16	98.1	0.3	0.9	0.6	97.7	0.2	1.0	1.1
Nov-16	98.8	0.3	0.5	0.4	98.2	0.3	0.8	0.8
Dec-16	98.7	0.3	0.6	0.4	97.1	0.3	1.2	1.4
Average	**92.2**	**3.8**	**2.9**	**1.1**	**94.8**	**2.7**	**1.6**	**0.9**
Standard deviation	**3.92**	**2.17**	**2.17**	**0.57**	**3.04**	**1.98**	**1.06**	**0.73**

Source: MSEI.

Product-wise shares in the currency derivatives volume show that the USD-INR options emerged as a dominant product with 48.7 percent share in turnover at NSE. On the other hand, at BSE and MSEI, USD-INR futures had major shares of 56.3 and 93.0 percent respectively.

Findings and Conclusions

1) During 2016-17, the total turnover was the highest at NSE (48, 57,076 crore), followed by BSE (18, 07,829 crore) and MSEI (2, 97,928 crore). NSE accounted for 69.8 percent of the total turnover in the currency segment followed by BSE (26.0 percent) and MSEI (4.3 percent).

2) Globally, currency derivatives' volumes have increased significantly since 2005, with a 10.4 percent increase in volumes traded in 2016 over the previous calendar year.

3) NSE was the second exchange in the world in currency derivatives in terms of the number of contracts traded in both futures and options segments (As per the WFE's 2016 report).

4) The increase in volume traded in Asia-Pacific region in 2016 was mainly driven by an increase in volumes at BSE (23 percent) and NSE (22 percent).

5) Product-wise shares in the currency derivatives volume show that the USD-INR options emerged as a dominant product with 48.7 percent share in turnover at NSE. On the other hand, at BSE and MSEI, USD-INR futures had major shares of 56.3 and 93.0 percent respectively.

Limitations of the Study

1. The study restricts itself to currency derivatives segment at the NSE only, even though there are other exchanges like MCX-SX, USE trading currency derivatives.

2. The data considered for this study is just for 5 years.

Scope for Further Study

The correlation between open interest and contracts traded at NSE in CD segment should be studied more carefully.

Further, researchers can test the currency futures for exchange rate volatility using econometric techniques such as Augment Dickey Fuller Test, cointegration methods.

References

Chowdary, M (2012). Three years of Currency Futures. *FICCI-Banking and Finance Digest*, 01-04.

Mathur, N (2012). Changing dynamics of Forex trade in India- OTC to Currency derivatives. *FICCI-Banking and Finance Digest*, 05-08.

Sarang VK (2012). *Evolution of Currency Futures Trading and its impact on Exchange rate Volatility in India (2000-2012).* www.investorsareidiots.com.

Sarma, S (2011). An Empirical Analysis of the Relationship Between Currency futures And exchange rates volatility in India. *RBI working paper series* .

SEBI. (2010). *Comparative study of currency futures versus OTC Currency market.* Mumbai: www.sebi.gov.in.

Srinivasan, S. (2012). Aiming for Quantum Growth in the FX Derivatives Market in India. *FICCI- Banking and Finance Digest*, 09-12.

Upadhyay, D. (2009). Currency Futures in India. *Management Insight* , 88-95.

Chapter 3

An Overview of the Foreign Exchange Market in India

G.Santhoshi Kumari,
Assistant Professor,
Noble Institute of Science and Technology,
Visakhapatnam.
Email: santhoshigondesi@gmail.com

Dr.M.S.V. Prasad,
Associate Professor, Head,
Department of Finance,
GITAM Institute of Management,
GITAM University, Visakhapatnam.
Email: msv@gitam.edu

Introduction

After the independence of India, 'Foreign Exchange Regulation Act (FERA)' was introduced as a temporary measure to regulate the inflow of the foreign capital. But with the economic and industrial development, the need for conservation of foreign currency was felt and on the recommendation of the Public Accounts Committee, the Indian government passed the Foreign Exchange Regulation Act 1973. Gradually, this act has been renamed as 'Foreign Exchange Management Act (FEMA)'. The Foreign Exchange Market in India operates under the Central Government of India and executes wide powers to control transactions in foreign exchange. The Foreign Exchange Management Act 1999 or FEMA regulates the whole foreign exchange market in India.

Before the introduction of this Act, the foreign exchange market in India was regulated by the Reserve Bank of India through the Exchange Control Department, by the Foreign Exchange Regulation Act or FERA, 1947. Up until 1992-93, the government exercised absolute control on the exchange rate, export-import policy, FDI (Foreign Direct Investment) policy.

Before 1992, the Reserve Bank of India (RBI) strictly controlled the exchange rate. This created a parallel foreign exchange market – a black market in foreign exchange popularly known as the "Hawala Market", which was an illegal foreign exchange market where Forex trading happened at a different rate than the rate mandated by the RBI. When the official rate "overvalues" the home currency, the "Hawala market" was operating in India before liberalization.

Post liberalization, the Government of India, felt the necessity to liberalize the foreign exchange policy. Hence, Foreign Exchange Management Act (FEMA) 2000 was introduced. FEMA expanded the list of activities in which a person/company can undertake Forex transactions. Through FEMA, the government liberalized the export-import policy, limits of FDI (Foreign Direct Investment) and FII (Foreign Institutional Investors) investments and repatriations, cross-border fundraising activities.

Foreign exchange market

A foreign exchange market refers to buying foreign currencies with domestic currencies and selling foreign currencies for domestic currencies. Thus, it is a market in which the claims to foreign monies are bought and sold for domestic currency. Exporters sell foreign currencies for domestic currencies and importers buy foreign currencies with domestic currencies. According to Ellsworth (1950)[1], "A Foreign Exchange Market comprises of all those institutions and individuals who buy and sell foreign exchange which may be defined as foreign money or any liquid claim on foreign money". Foreign exchange transactions result in the inflow and outflow of currency of a country.

Functions of foreign exchange market

Foreign exchange is also referred to as Forex market. Participants are importers, exporters, tourists and investors, traders and speculators, commercial banks, brokers and central banks. Foreign bill of exchange, telegraphic transfer, bank draft, letter of credit, etc. are the important foreign exchange instruments used in the foreign exchange market to carry out its functions. The foreign exchange market performs the following functions.

1. **Transfer of Purchasing Power and Clearing Function:** The basic function of the foreign exchange market is to facilitate the conversion of one currency into another i.e. payment between exporters and importers. For example, the Indian rupee is converted into U.S. dollar and vice-versa. To perform the transfer function variety of credit, instruments are used such as telegraphic transfers, bank drafts and foreign bills. Telegraphic transfer is the quickest method of transferring amount.

---

[1] Ellsworth P.T. (1950), The International Economy, New York, Macmillan.

2. **Credit Function:** The foreign exchange market also provides credit to both national and international, to promote foreign trade. It is necessary as international payments sometimes get delayed for 60 or 90 days. Obviously, when foreign bills of exchange are used in international payments, a credit for about 3 months, till its maturity, is required.

3. **Hedging Function:** A third function of the foreign exchange market is to hedge foreign exchange risks. By hedging, we mean covering of a foreign exchange risk arising out of the changes in exchange rates. Under this function, the foreign exchange market tries to protect the interest of the persons dealing in the market from any unforeseen changes in exchange rate. The exchange rates under a free market can go up and down; this can either bring gains or losses to concerned parties. Hedging guards the interest of both exporters as well as importers, against any changes in exchange rate. Hedging can be done either by means of a spot exchange market or a forward exchange market involving a forward contract.

Participants and dealers in the foreign exchange market

The foreign exchange market needs dealers to facilitate foreign exchange transactions. Bulks of foreign exchange transaction are dealt with by commercial banks and financial institutions. RBI has also allowed private authorized dealers to deal with foreign exchange transactions, i.e., buying and selling foreign currency. The main participants in foreign exchange markets are:

- **Retail Clients:** Retail clients deal through commercial banks and authorized agents. They comprise people, international investors, multinational corporations and others who need foreign exchange.

- **Commercial Banks:** Commercial banks carry out buying and selling orders from their retail clients. They deal with other commercial banks and also through foreign exchange brokers.

- **Foreign Exchange Brokers:** Each foreign exchange market centre has some authorized brokers. The Brokers act as intermediaries between buyers and sellers, mainly for banks. Commercial banks prefer these brokers.

- **Central Banks**: Under floating exchange rate the central bank does not interfere in the exchange market. Since 1973, most of the central banks intervened to buy and sell currencies to influence the rate at which currencies are traded.

Types of foreign exchange market

The foreign exchange market is composed of retail and wholesale markets.

1. **Retail Market:** The retail market is a secondary price maker. Travellers, tourists and people who need foreign exchange for permitted small transactions, exchange one currency for another.

2. **Wholesale Market:** The wholesale market is also called Interbank Market. The size of transactions in this market is very large. Dealers are highly professionals and are primary price makers. The main participants are commercial banks, business corporations and central banks. Multinational banks are mainly responsible for determining the exchange rate.

3. **Other Participants**

   a) **Brokers:** Brokers have more information and better knowledge of markets. They provide information to banks about the prices at which there are buyers and sellers of a pair of currencies.

   b) **Price Takers:** Price takers are those who buy foreign exchange which they require and sell what they earn at the price determined by primary price makers.

Foreign exchange market India

The FX market plays a significant role in global trade by determining the strength of an economy and its growth. The world has moved into from a transition of foreign exchange practices after Bretton Woods in 1944, and then from a fixed to flexible exchange rate regime in 1972. During this period, India has been following the global practices moving from peg exchange rate regime to a floating rate exchange system and IS currently following a market based exchange system. Even though, the Indian exchange rate is being controlled by the Reserve Bank of India (RBI). Global FX market comprises of the spot market, the forward market, the future market, and the options in the derivatives market segment. In India during August 2008 the first foreign currency trading system was introduced against the US dollar, then the Euro, the British Pound Sterling and the Japanese Yen in the National Stock Exchange of India (NSE), later in the Multi-Commodity Exchange of India for currency trading (MCX-SX), and Bombay Stock Exchange of India (BSE). Now exclusive exchange started by BSE in the name of United Stock Exchange of India (USE).

This paved the way for the foreign exchange payments/receipts to be converted at the market-determined exchange rate. Convertibility in current account means that individuals and companies have the freedom to buy or sell foreign currency on specific activities like foreign travel, medical expenses, college fees, as well as for payment/receipt related to export-import, interest payment/receipt, investment in foreign securities, business expenses, etc. A related concept to this is the "convertibility in capital account", which indicates that Indian people and business houses can freely convert rupee to any other currency to any extent and can invest in foreign assets like shares, real estate in foreign countries. Most importantly, Indian banks can accept deposits in any currency (Balakrishnan, 2009).

The Role of the Foreign Exchange Market

The foreign exchange (Forex) market is the world's biggest financial market by far. According to the Bank for International Settlements' (BIS) triennial survey, global Forex turnover in April 2010 averaged a staggering $4.0 trillion daily, an increase of 20% from $3.3 trillion three years earlier. In a globalized economy, the significance of the foreign exchange marketplace to the average consumer cannot be underestimated. The rate at which our domestic currency can be exchanged in the global Forex market determines the price we pay for an increasing number of products, the price tag for our vacations, the rate of return on our investments (ROI) and even the interest rate on our loans and deposits.

Transactions in the foreign exchange market can be broadly classified into two types: – commercial and speculative. A commercial transaction is one that is backed by an underlying economic activity, such as payment for an import or a loan to an overseas entity. A speculative transaction, on the other hand, is one undertaken purely to make a profit from currency moves. Speculative transactions greatly exceed commercial transactions in the realm of foreign exchange, and they have accounted for a greater share of Forex trading volumes over the years. Also, currency trading volume in the 1970s was only about six times the value of global trade in goods and services. But by 1995, daily Forex trading volume of $1.2 trillion was approximately 50 times this value.

Forex trading volume has increased more than threefold since then, driven largely by speculation. A study based on the 2010 BIS survey found that the ratio of Forex turnover to gross domestic product (GDP) – a good measure of speculative activity – ranged from about 14 percent for the United States and Japan to 200 percent for the United Kingdom and more than 300 percent for Singapore. Also, despite the 20 percent increase in daily Forex volumes between 2007 and 2010, commercial transactions by corporations and governments actually declined by 10% over this period. Commercial transactions accounted for only 13 percent of daily total Forex volume in 2010, the lowest share since 2001.Online Forex trading by retail investors has grown enormously since 2007, with such transactions contributing to about $125 billion to $150 billion in daily Forex turnover. The lure of making money by speculating on exchange rate movements is obviously a powerful one (Sivarajadhanavel and Kumaramangalam, 2012).

Pitfalls in the Foreign Exchange Market

For retail Forex trader, the biggest risk of non-regulation is that of illegal activity or outright fraud. Following are the limitation of foreign exchange market

- **Heightened Volatility**: The surge in speculative activity, especially high-frequency trading dominated by computerized or algorithmic trading, may contribute to higher currency volatility, which increases the risk of runaway losses for the small investor or trader.

- **Information Disadvantage:** Retail investors are at a distinct disadvantage in the largely unregulated global Forex market since they do not have access to information about large commercial transactions and capital flows only available to the biggest players who dominate the market. This information unevenness makes it difficult for the average retail investor to gain any type of advantage over professionals.

- **Higher Hedging Costs**: Increased currency volatility caused by excessive speculation leads to higher costs incurred by corporations and other commercial players for hedging currency risk.

- **Systemic Importance of Big Banks:** While Forex trading losses were not prominent in the biggest trading losses posted by corporations and financial institutions to date, the potential does exist for billion-dollar losses on wrong currency bets. Although currency trading is a zero-sum game, a massive loss incurred by a big bank could have a ripple effect on the global economy due to its systemic importance.

- **Undue Enrichment of a Few at the Expense of Millions:** Exaggerated or unjustified currency moves can adversely affect a nation's economy. Although such moves may be justified by underlying economic fundamentals in some cases, in many other cases temporary weakness in a currency can be exploited ruthlessly by speculators, sending it into freefall in a self-fulfilling prophecy. This can trigger capital flight and a prolonged recession precipitated by sharply higher interest rates to defend the currency. This scenario has played out on several occasions over the past two decades; a notable instance being the collapse of the Thai baht in July 1997 and the subsequent Asian crisis. While currency speculators raked in the profits, millions of people in the affected nations suffered huge wealth erosion and long periods of unemployment.

Conclusion

Liberalization has transformed India's external sector and a direct beneficiary has been the foreign exchange market in India. From a foreign exchange-starved, control-ridden economy, India has moved on to a position of $150 billion plus in international reserves with a confident rupee and drastically reduced foreign exchange control. As foreign trade and cross-border capital flows continue to grow, and the country moves towards capital account convertibility, the foreign exchange market is poised to play an even greater role in the economy. However, it is unlikely to be completely free of RBI interventions any time soon.

References

Balakrishnan.S (2009), Forex Speculation Drives Corporate Losses, Business Line, February 14th.

Ellsworth P.T. (1950), *The International Economy, New York, Macmillan.*

Sivarajadhanavel P and Chandra Kumaramangalam S., (2012). Exchange Rate Risk in the Foreign Exchange Market: A Challenge on Corporate Profitability. *International Journal of Industrial Engineering and Management Science,* ISSN 2277 – 5056, Bonfring, 2(3).

Triennial Central Bank Survey December 2007: Foreign exchange and derivatives market activity in 2007.http://www.bis.org/publ/rpfxf07t.pdf

Chapter 4

Pareto Currency Risk Management Strategy - A Passive Hedge

Dr.K. Bhanu Prakash,
Associate Professor,
V ESTAL Institutions, Eluru.
Mobile No.: +91-9440321648.

Dr. Chowdary Venu Gopal,
Assistant Professor,
GITAM University, Bengaluru.
Mobile No.: +91-9440710959
Email: drchowdary959@gmail.com

Introduction

The US\$ is a central currency due to liquidity and stability. More than 85% of daily Forex transactions are done in US\$. After Demonetization in India, the 'Indian Rupee' *(INR)* has become stronger than currencies of 143 economies. Since the beginning of 2017, the INR has increased by nearly 4 % against the US\$ and in cross-currency trades, the INR ended higher against the Pound Sterling at 86.86 on 18th Sep, 2017. It can be observed that there is a currency risk in the long or short term and the policies to hedge or avoid are a prime concern.

Global Currency Markets - The Trends and Trajectories

The US\$ has been a *theme du jour* for global investors since the bull market began in the mid-1990s.[1] The direction of the US\$ is a matter of concern for global equity market investors as it affects the valuation of stocks and impacts the variables like: (i) earnings growth; (ii) interest rates; and (iii) the risk premium. The price of the dollar fell on the international market, headed for the biggest weekly gain, more than halved its daily loss and was on track for the strongest weekly advance since February 2017. Consumer inflation expecta-

---

[1] Shaun K. Roache and Matthew D. Merritt (2006). Currency Risk Premia in Global Stock Markets, IMF Working Paper, P/06/194.

tions rose from the prior month as investor focus began turning to next week's Federal Reserve Policy Meeting. The pound surged to a Post-Brexit high as BOE's Vlieghe turned hawkish and the Sterling rallied to take the shine off the Dollar. The sterling climbed to its highest level versus the Dollar since Brexit, the Yen fell against all G-10 peers, as missile fatigue set in (in other words a sudden fall in the market turnover), as on the trading date of 15th Sep, 2017, according to Bloomberg Currencies Market.

Figure 4.1: Bloomberg currency market index.

The Foreign Exchange (FOREX) Market is the world's largest and most liquid market with trillions of dollars traded on any given day between millions of parties. The US ($) is the most traded currency (85%) and the Euro (EUR 33.40%) has become the second most traded and the world's second largest reserve currency. The Japanese Yen (JPY, 23%) is the third most traded currency followed by the British Pound (GBP, 11.8%), the Australian Dollar (AUD 8.6%), the Swiss Franc (CHF, 5.2%), the Canadian Dollar (CAD 4.6%), the Mexican Peso (MXN 2.5%), the Chinese Yuan Renminbi (CNY 2.2%) and the New Zealand Dollar (NZD 1.40%). The major Traded Pairs of Currencies in the world are EUR/USD, USD/JPY, GBP/USD, AUD/USD, USD/CHF, NZD/USD and USD/CAD and the most popular Cross Rates are EUR/JPY, EUR/GBP, EUR/CHF, GBP/JPY and GBP/CHF. The GBP/USD is known as the 'Cable'. The total volume of transactions in Forex Market was $ 40,143 million on a Trade Date of 15th Sep, 2017. In the month of August, the total volume was $622,742 million with Average Daily Volume (ADV) of $27,076 million. The quarterly results show that in the Q1 of 2017, the total volume of transactions in Forex market was $1,872,701 million with ADV of $$28,811. However, there is a fall in the total volume of transactions ($1,815,228 million) and ADV ($27,927 million) in Q2 of 2017.[2]

Currency risk also termed foreign exchange risk as the risk that a long or short position in a foreign currency might have to be closed out at a loss due to an adverse movement in exchange rates.[3] Currency risk can be observed by the historic volatility and examining currency rate forecasts. The policies to hedge or avoid currency risks are: (i) shifting the risk to others; (ii) improving productivity and reducing costs; (iii) structural hedging and (iv) hedging with treasury instruments.[4]

Figure 4.2: Base Currency (INR) Versus Quote / Counter Currency (USD, EUR, JPY, GBP) During 2008-09 to 2017-18. (Until the 18th Sep, 2017).

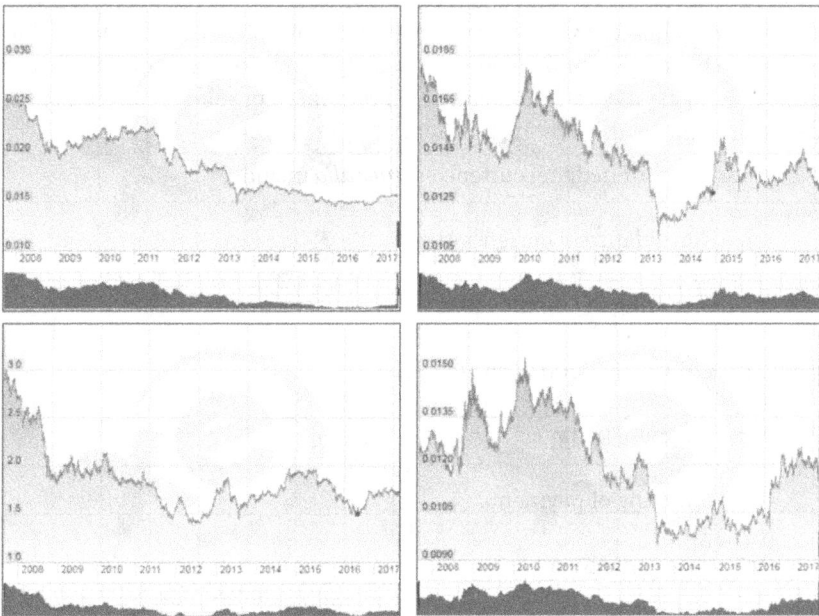

Source: www.xe.com

After Demonetization, INR has become stronger than the currencies of 143 countries. Since the beginning of 2017, the INR has risen by nearly 4 %

---

[2] https://www.hotspotfx.com/products/hotspot_volumes.jsp
[3] http://www.nasdaq.com/investing/glossary/f/foreign-exchange-risk
[4] Brian Coyle (2000). *Hedging Currency Exposures: Currency Risk Management*, Financial World Publications, UK, 17-18.

against the US\$[5] and remained higher as it was recorded at 64.05 on 18th Sep 2017. The value of Indian rupee had gained by 0.04 paise[6] or 0.06% against the US\$ on the previous Friday. In cross-currency trades, the INR ended higher against the Pound Sterling at 86.86 but fell against the Euro to finish at 76.71as on 18th Sep 2017.[7]

Strategies for Hedging of Currencies

The suspension of gold conversion window in 1971 was the dawn of the Modern currency market and according to the Bank of International Settlements (BIS), over \$5T of currencies are transacted each day. US\$ is used as a central currency due to its liquidity and stability. Hence, 85% of all Forex transactions are done through the US\$. The volatility, uncertainty, complexity and ambiguity of general conditions and situations in Forex markets change the exposed positions of a company in one currency or in multiple currencies termed as Hedging.[8] It can also be defined as the taking of a position, acquiring a cash flow (CF), an asset, or a contract that will rise or fall in value to offset a fall or rise in the value of the existing position.[9]

The strategies for hedging currencies *inter alia* include:

   i.   avoidance of currency risk;

   ii.   sharing of currency risk;

   iii.   diversification of currency risk;

   iv.   natural hedging;

   v.   netting of payments;

   vi.   pre-payment;

   vii.   Leading and Lagging;

---

[5] Tushar Arora (2017). Explaining the sharp rise in the Rupee, *The Business Line*, 28th Mar.
[6] One Indian Rupee equal to 100 paise.
[7] http://economictimes.indiatimes.com/articleshow/60734634.cms?utm_source=conte ntofinterestandutm_ medium = textandutm_campaign=cppst
[8] Prindl, A.R. (1976). *Foreign Exchange Risk*, Wiley, London.
[9] William Fung and David. A. Hsieh (2004), Hedge Funds Bench Marks - A Risk Based Approach, Journal *of Financial Analysts*, 58(5) 65-80.

   viii.   Cross Hedging;

   ix.   Parallel Loan (Back-to-Back Loan);

   x.   Overseas Loan / Foreign Currency-Denominated Debt;

   xi.   Insurance;

   xii.   Money Market Hedge;

   xiii.   Borrowing Policy;

   xiv.   Pricing Strategy and

   xv.   Derivative Instruments.

Currency derivatives can reduce the risk in currency transactions and these include (a) currency forwards; (b) currency futures; (c) currency options and (d) currency Swaps. A practical strategy for cutting down of currency costs is by hedging. There are different kinds of hedging strategies, but a forward contract is a popular method that sets a current rate for future use.[10]

The Pareto currency risk management strategy - an overview

The Pareto CRM Strategy is a quantitative overlay strategy designed for institutional investors to manage foreign currency risk resulting from translation exposure. The prime objective is restructuring the distribution of currency returns. This is achieved by targeting an optimal hedge Ratio per foreign currency by systematically measuring and combining the (i) econometric valuation, (ii) interest rate differentials, (iii) momentum and (iv) volatility; keeping in view risk constraints. The Pareto CRM strategy is similar to portfolio insurance or purchasing option protection designed to deliver a similar pay-off at a lower cost.

---

[10] Alex Bennett (2017). Currency Strategies to Minimize Costs and Mitigate Risks in the Aviation Industry, Credit Control, p.48.

Table 4.1: Individual Currency Hedging Positions during 2016-17.

Currency	July, 2017	Jan, 2017	July, 2016
CAD	31%	51%	42%
CHF	76%	65%	60%
EUR	54%	56%	56%
GBP	64%	61%	61%
JPY	56%	54%	20%
USD	63%	47%	46%
AGG	61%	51%	47%

Source: Insight Investment, Aug 2017, p.1.

The major contributing factors to CRM's Current Positioning are: (i) US$, (ii) CHF and GBP and (iii) CAD. The aggregate hedge level was 61% which masks a reduction in the CAD Hedge to 31% from 51% and an increase in the GBP hedge from 48% to 64%. Over the medium-term, CRM has outperformed a passively held hedge; the representative CRM portfolio is 30bp and 16bp per annum above the passive benchmark over 3 and 5 years respectively.

Table 4.2: Factors Attribution of Representative CRM Portfolio - A Passive Hedge (50%).

	Volatility	Momentum	Carry	Value	Total
CAD	0.3%	-1.3%	0.2%	-0.4%	-1.3%
CHF	0.1%	-0.8%	2.9%	-2.6%	-0.4%
EUR	-0.1%	-0.4%	0.6%	-0.8%	-0.7%
GBP	-0.6%	0.6%	2.0%	-3.0%	-0.9%
JPY	0.1%	-0.1%	2.2%	-3.4%	-1.3%
USD	0.0%	-0.5%	0.2%	0.3%	0.1%
AGG	0.0%	-0.4%	0.7%	-0.6%	-0.3%

Source: Insight Investment, 30th June 2017.

Conclusion

Risk is a precarious element of investing and monitoring, measuring and managing currency. Changes in interest rates, inflation and trade are the 3-

drivers of currency valuation in short-run. Central banks control short-term interest rates, which in turn exert a strong influence over inflation, thereby pivotal to currency valuation.

The currency risk management prudent strategies *viz.*, hedge accounting, hedging foreign currency transactions, forward Contracts, flexible forward transactions, FX options and currency swaps *etc.*, depending on the purpose and stability. It is suggested to identify a suitable risk and customized management strategy to mitigate the threat of currency risk. While spot or forward contracts are sufficient for the hedging, more sophisticated products such as 'Options' can help to meet short-term fluctuations in Forex rates and their impact on payables and receivables.

This paper suggests that smart hedging strategies can reduce the currency risks in emerging markets besides the streamlining of the best global payment systems. Despite the volatility nature of the markets, *currency costs* can also be managed to some degree in order to minimize losses and mitigate currency exchange risk.

Hence, the Pareto currency risks management strategy with a hedging option which reduces currency risk and improves financial stability over time. It also increases the probability of achieving investment objectives in medium and long-term.

References

Bartram, P. (2015). How to Manage Foreign Exchange Currency Risk, Director, Mar, p.70.

Bennett, A. (2017). Currency Strategies to Minimize Costs and Mitigate Risks in the Aviation Industry, Credit Control, p.48.

Coyle, B. (2000). Hedging Currency Exposures: Currency Risk Management, Financial World Publications, UK, 17-18.

Fung, W. and Hsieh, D. A. (2004), Hedge Funds Bench Marks - A Risk Based Approach, Journal of Financial Analysts, 58(5) 65-80.

Mishler, M. D. (2017). Currency turmoil, price, and profit in global markets: How to manage the risks of volatile foreign currency exchange rates, Journal of Accountancy, pp.1-7.

O'Brien, T. J. (2017). Applied International Finance I: Managing Foreign Exchange Risk, Second Edition, Business Expert Press, New York.

Población García, F. J (2017). Financial Risk Management: Identification, Measurement and Management, Palgrave MacMillan, Frankfurt, Germany.

Prindl, A. R. (1976). Foreign Exchange Risk, Wiley, London.

Roache, S. K. and Merritt, M. D. (2006). Currency Risk Premia in Global Stock Markets, IMF Working Paper, P/06/194, p.3.

Robson, B. (2017). Currency Kings: How Billionaire Traders Made their Fortune Trading Forex and How You Can Too, McGraw Hill Professional, USA.

Sivakumar, A. and Sarkar, R. (2016). Corporate Hedging for Foreign Exchange Risk in India, IIT Kharagpur, Working Paper, 1-17.

Tushar, A. (2017). Explaining the sharp rise in the Rupee, The Business Line, 28th Mar.

Chapter 5

A Study on Price Discovery
of Currency Futures at NSE

Satyanarayana Koilada,
Assistant professor,
Noble Institute of Science and Technology,
Lankelapalem, Visakhapatnam.
Email: justsatya@gmail.com

Haniefuddin Sk,
Director,
Noble Institute of Science and Technology,
Lankelapalem, Visakhapatnam.
Email: haniefuddin@rediffmail.com

Introduction

The foreign exchange market is the world's largest market in terms of trade value and was estimated at $5.09 trillion (Bank for International Settlements) in the year 2016. It is important to note that as the market grows bigger, the foreign exchange management gains significance. Foreign exchange trading in India was introduced in the year when Reserve Bank of India allowed banks to undertake intraday trading in the foreign exchange segment. A foreign exchange rate is highly volatile and responds to all global factors directly and indirectly. The international trading community has a greater interest in foreign exchange rates since their business is significantly affected by the exchange rates. A currency derivative comes in handy for the traders and can be used as a tool for mitigating future exchange rate risk.

Currency derivatives in India launched at the national stock exchange with the introduction of currency futures against USD in the year 2008 and subsequently was allowed to trade against other strong currencies like EURO, POUND and YEN. Though the magnitude of exchange traded currency derivatives against over the counter trade is very small, the currency derivatives are exceptionally doing well at NSE F&O segment. Total traded turnover of Currency derivatives at NSE for the year 2016 stood at Rs 48, 57,075 Cr. with the average daily turnover of Rs 19,394.83 Cr.

Figure 5.1: Growth of Currency Derivatives at NSE Since Inception in Rs. Cr.

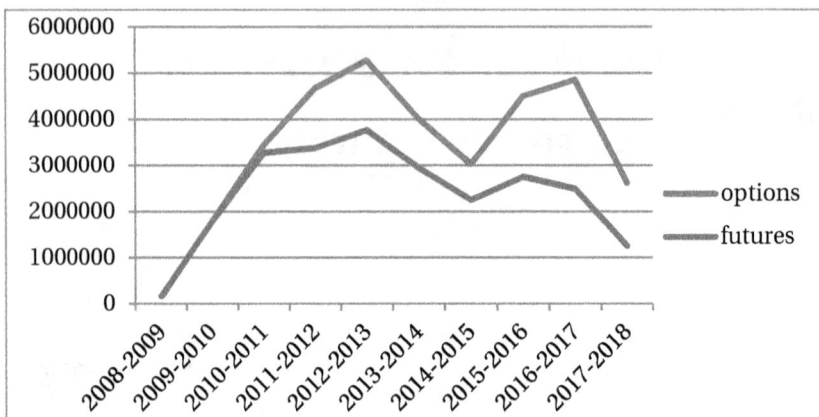

Source: WWW.NSEINDIA.COM

The World Federation of Exchanges reports that the currency derivative trade volume increased significantly during the period of 2015-2016 in both futures and options. While the market increased in the North American region by 14% during this period, the Asia-Pacific region witnessed a tremendous growth rate of 23% which was driven by BSE and NSE with a growth rate of 23% and 22% respectively.

Table 5.1: Changes in Currency Options and Futures 2015-2016.

	2015	2016	% change	% of total (asset class)	% of total (overall)
Currency Options		650	39.3%	18%	3%
Currency Futures	2 115	2 199	4.0%	82%	9%
Total Currency	2 581	2 850	10.4%		11%

Source: World Federation of Exchanges (WFE).

Table 5.2: Top 10 currency contracts traded in 2016.

	Contract Name	Exchange	Volume		Notional Value		Open Interest	
			2016	AGR	2016	AGR	2016	AGR
1	USD/RUB futures	Moscow Exchange	865 068 634	-4%	980 880	26%	2 626 442	-10%
2	USDINR Options	NSE India Ltd	351 632 420	63%	351 609	66%	NA	NA
3	USDINR Futures	NSE India Ltd.	351 162 981	-2%	349 620	0%	NA	NA
4	USDINR Futures	BSE Ltd.	319 413 292	24%	NA	NA	NA	NA
5	USDINR Options	BSE Ltd.	207 386 529	22%	NA	NA	NA	NA
6	Mini U.S. Dollar Futures	BM& FBOVESPA	92 119 754	NA	981 794	NA	508 417	NA
7	U.S. Dollar Futures	BM& FBOVESPA	71 281 293	-8%	3 832 059	16%	13 388 898	1059%
8	EURO FX	CME Group	49 455 909	-24%	6 848 045	-32%	408 748	2%
9	USD Futures	Korea Exchange	56 869 526	8%	54 775 617	10692%	777 433	27%
10	JAPANESE YEN futures	CME Group	36 588 788	1%	4 201 948	12%	212 942	4%

Source: World Federation of Exchanges (WFE).

With the constant changes by international businesses, traders are in need of efficient foreign exchange management. Currency derivatives are complex and yet powerful risk management tools and applied heavily in foreign exchange management. It provides several benefits to the market participants such as hedging, arbitrage opportunities, and investment leverage.

Literature Review

Since the currency futures market facilitates an advantage for the investor through marginal investment, many researchers argue that the informational investors would opt for the futures market over spot market. Thus, currency futures market would attract all the informed traders and rates are adjusted accordingly. This would further lead the spot market exchange rates. Contrary to this argument, some researchers advise that the present currency needs to be settled in cash hence the currency demand and supply would be absorbed into the spot rates. The study documents the finding of a survey of brokers' perception after introducing the commodity derivatives market in India (Osler et al. 2011)[1]. The survey results show the brokers' assessment of trading/marketing activities and their perception of the benefits and concerns about commodity derivatives. It also throws some light on the perception of brokers about the efficiency of Indian commodity derivatives in performing the functions of price discovery, hedging effectiveness and volatility dynamics.

Another article outlined that the UK contribution to BIS and focus largely changes in FX markets. Many studies have examined the relationship between currency spot and futures markets (Hasbrouck, 1995)[2].

Chan's[3] study provides evidence that this price discovery process cannot be based on adverse selection between dealers and their customers, as postulated in standard models because the spreads dealers quote to their customers are not positively related to a trade's likely information content.

Sehgal et al. (2015) analysed dynamic interdependence via growth spillovers between financial cycles represented by real bank credit growth and business cycle as real GDP growth and also examined the price discovery and volatility spillovers in spot and futures.[4]

The current study aims to examine the causal relationship between the NSE currency future rates and currency spot rates in order to identify the price discovery mechanism at NSE market and its integration with foreign exchange market (spot market). To study the causal relationship between the said markets, we have considered daily closing rates for NSE currency futures and currency spot rates for selected pairs of currencies, i.e., USD/INR, GBP/INR, JPY/INR and EURO/INR. The data was obtained from www.nseindia.com and www.investing.com for the period from Jan-2010 to Sep-2017 which makes it

---

[1] Osler, C. L., Mende, A., & Menkhoff, L. (2011). Price discovery in currency markets. *Journal of International Money and Finance, 30*(8), 1696-1718.

[2] Hasbrouck, J. (1995), "One security, many markets: determining the contributions to price discovery", Journal of Finance, Vol. 50 No. 4, pp. 1175-1199.

[3] Chan K. (1992). A further analysis of the lead-lag relationship between the cash market and stock index futures market. Review of Financial Studies, 5(1), 123–152.

[4] Sehgal, S., Ahmad, W., & Deisting, F. (2015), Business Cycle and Financial cycle Interdependence, Journal of Quantative economics, June 2018, Volume 16, Issue 2, pp 337–362.

approximately 1750 observations for each currency pair in each market (Srivasatava and Sigh, 2015)[5].

Sakthivel, Chittedi, & Sakyi (2017) observed that the spot market adjusts to new information faster than futures market suggesting that spot price leads the futures price and contributes largely to price discovery the results of the study show that there is unidirectional volatility transmission from currency spot to futures prices of JPY/INR, GBP/INR and EUR/INR and bidirectional spillover between currency spot and futures prices of USD/INR. Based on the findings, relevant policy recommendations are made.

Price discovery could be referred to as the use of the futures price to discover the prices existing in the spot market, which further depends upon the strength of the relationship between the prices of the futures contracts and their underlying. The following study is aimed at investigating the relationship between the spot rates of INR-USD, INR-GBP, INR-Euro and INR-Yen exchange rates and the futures contracts for the same pairs traded in Indian financial markets.[6]

The study of Gonzalo (1995) consisted of the competitiveness and their connection with real exchange rate misalignments. It will then summarize a range of methodologies available for assessing real exchange misalignments, outlining potential obstacles and providing some suggestions for how these can be overcome.[7] The study did not test the convergence empirically but observed the pattern of trading and the study on market efficiency in India supports the dependency of two on each other, i.e., there is a long run stable relationship between foreign currency spot and futures market.

Many studies have examined the relationship between currency spot and futures markets. The majority of studies suggest that the futures lead the spot prices (Stoll and Whaley, 1990[8]; Kawaller, Koch and Koch, 1987)[9]while some have advised otherwise. In the foreign exchange market, the currency futures market

[5] Srivastava, A. and Singh, M. (2015), "A study on pricing of currency futures in Indian currency market", International Journal of Research in Finance and Marketing, Vol. 5 No. 6, pp. 1-11.

[6] De Boyrie, M.E., Pavlova, I. and Parhizgari, A.M. (2012), "Price discovery in currency markets: evidence from three emerging markets", International Journal of Economics and Finance, Vol. 4 No. 12, pp. 12-61.

[7] Gonzalo, J. and Granger, C. (1995), "Estimation of common long-memory components in cointegrated systems", Journal of Business and Economic Statistics, Vol. 13 No. 1, pp. 27-35.

[8] Hans R. Stoll and Robert E. Whaley (1990). The Dynamics of Stock Index and Stock Index Futures Returns. *The Journal of Financial and Quantitative Analysis,*25(4), 441-468.

[9] Ira G. Kawaller, Paul D. Koch and Timothy W. Koch (1987). The Temporal Price Relationship Between S&P 500 Futures and the S&P 500 Index. *The Journal of Finance*, 42(5), 1309-1329.

share is much smaller than the currency spot market and it is argued that the significance of currency futures in determining spot rate is even less (Lyons, 2001)[10]. However, the 2007 BIS Triennial survey suggested that the currency futures market plays a significant role in the price discovery process compared to the spot market. Kharbanda and Singh (2017)[11] examined the lead-lag relationship between NSE currency futures rates and spot currency rates using daily closing rates under a VECM model and concluded that the future rates lead the spot rates. It is also found that the futures lead spot in all pairs of currencies available at NSE, i.e., USD/INR, GBP/INR, JPY/INR and EURO/INR.

The Granger Causality Test is an appropriate method of identifying the lead-lag relationship between the time series data. It is necessary to have the variables stationarity in order to proceed further to test the Granger Causality. Hence, we applied the Augmented Dicky Fuller test in order to test the stationarity of the data. Table 5.3 summarizes the results from the ADF.

The below test result exhibits that all the future rates and spot rates at level are nonstationary since the 'p' values are greater than .05 which fails to reject the null hypothesis of the unit root (Non-stationarity). The variables at first difference are found to be stationary since the p value is less than .05 and rejecting the null hypothesis of non-stationarity. Since the variables are at level, i.e. without any order of difference found nonstationary, it cannot be applied in Granger causality Test. Therefore, the variables at first difference can be used in testing the Granger Causality Test.

Table 5.3: ADF test of NONSTATIONARITY.

Null Hypothesis: Unit root (individual unit root process)
Series: DEURFUT, DEURSPOT, DGBPFUT, DGBPSPOT, DJPYFUT, DJPYSPOT, DUSDFUT, DUSDSPOT, EURFUT, EUROSPOT, GBPFUT, GBPSPOT, JPYFUT, JPYSPOT, USDFUT, USDSPOT
Sample: 1/01/2010 10/18/2017
Exogenous variables: Individual effects
Automatic selection of maximum lags
Automatic lag length selection based on AIC: 1 to 9
Total number of observations: 24170
Cross-sections included: 16

[10] Lyons, Richard K. (2001). The Microstructure Approach to Exchange Rates. MIT Press, Cambridge, MA.

[11] Varuna Kharbanda and Archana Singh, (2017). Lead-lag relationship between futures and spot FX market in India. *International Journal of Managerial Finance*, 13(5), 560-577.

Method	Statistic	Prob.**
ADF - Fisher Chi-square	1219.32	0.0000
ADF - Choi Z-stat	-23.3688	0.0000

** Probabilities for Fisher tests are computed using an asymptotic Chi -square distribution. All other tests assume asymptotic normality.

Intermediate ADF test results UNTITLED

Series	Prob.	Lag	Max Lag	Obs
DEURFUT	0.0000	3	9	1046
DEURSPOT	0.0000	4	25	2015
DGBPFUT	0.0000	1	9	1302
DGBPSPOT	0.0000	1	25	2031
DJPYFUT	0.0000	3	9	1046
DJPYSPOT	0.0000	1	25	2018
DUSDFUT	0.0000	8	9	596
DUSDSPOT	0.0000	1	25	2031
EURFUT	0.4946	4	9	1046
EUROSPOT	0.5433	5	25	2015
GBPFUT	0.6011	2	9	1302
GBPSPOT	0.5591	2	25	2031
JPYFUT	0.5470	4	9	1046
JPYSPOT	0.1810	2	25	2018
USDFUT	0.8896	9	9	596
USDSPOT	0.5591	2	25	2031

Granger Causality Test

The Granger Causality Test is applied for each pair of currency using first differenced data from both spot and futures markets. Table 5.4 exhibits the result from Granger Causality Test for EURO/INR spot and future rates and it implies that there is bi-directional causality between EURO/INR spot and futures markets since the p values for both hypotheses are less than .05 significance level and suggesting the rejection of null hypotheses.

Table 5.4: Granger Causality test for EURO/INR spot and future rate.

Pair wise Granger Causality Tests			
Sample: 1/01/2010 10/18/2017			
Lags: 2			
Null Hypothesis:	**Obs**	**F-Statistic**	**Prob.**
DEURSPOT does not Granger Cause DEURFUT	1293	197.312	0.00
DEURFUT does not Granger Cause DEURSPOT		10.8452	0.00

Table 5.5 exhibits the result from Granger Causality Test for GBP/INR spot and future rates. The system automatically selected the lag length of 2 using the Akaike Information Criterion (AIC) for the model estimation. The result implies that there is bi-directional causality between GBP/INR spot and futures markets since the p values for both hypotheses is less than 5% significance level and suggesting the rejection of null hypotheses.

Table 5.5: Granger Causality test for GBP/INR spot and future rate.

Pair wise Granger Causality Tests			
Sample: 1/01/2010 10/18/2017			
Lags: 2			
Null Hypothesis:	**Obs**	**F-Statistic**	**Prob.**
DGBPSPOT does not Granger Cause DGBPFUT	1302	103.319	0.00
DGBPFUT does not Granger Cause DGBPSPOT		21.8932	0.01

Table 5.6 exhibits the result from Granger Causality Test for JPY/INR spot and future rates and it implies that there is uni-directional causality from JPY/INR spot rates to future market rates since the p values for null hypothesis "DJPYSPOT does not Granger Cause DJPYFUT" is less than .05 significance level and suggesting the rejection of the null hypotheses. It signifies that JPY/INR future rate does not cause JPY/INR spot rate.

Table 5.6: Granger Causality test for JPY/INR spot and future rate.

Pair wise Granger Causality Tests			
Sample: 1/01/2010 10/18/2017			
Lags: 2			
Null Hypothesis:	**Obs**	**F-Statistic**	**Prob.**
DJPYSPOT does not Granger Cause DJPYFUT	1293	147.461	0.0011
DJPYFUT does not Granger Cause DJPYSPOT		0.18529	0.8309

Table 5.7 exhibits the result from Granger Causality Test for USD/INR spot and future rates and it implies that there is uni-directional causality from USD/INR futures rate to spot market rates since the p values for null hypothesis "DUSDFUT does not Granger Cause DUSDSPOT" is less than .05 significance level and suggesting the rejection of the null hypotheses. It signifies that USD/INR spot rate does not cause USD/INR future rate.

Table 5.7: Granger Causality test for USD/INR spot and future rate.

Pair wise Granger Causality Tests			
Sample: 1/01/2010 10/18/2017			
Lags: 2			
Null Hypothesis:	**Obs**	**F-Statistic**	**Prob.**
DUSDSPOT does not Granger Cause DUSDFUT	1319	0.43450	0.6477
DUSDFUT does not Granger Cause DUSDSPOT		3.58609	0.0280

Variance Decomposition

Although the causal relationship between spot and futures identified in the previous analysis, it does not disclose relative strength of the variables in the VAR system to the exogenous shocks. Variance decomposition is a method of identifying forecast error variance of each variable from a vector autoregressive (VAR) system. The results from this method are very sensitive to the ordering of variables which generally follows Cholesky's ordering. The Cholesky decomposition algorithm was first proposed by Andre-Louis Cholesky (October 15, 1875 - August 31, 1918)[12] at the end of the First World War. He was a

---

[12] Voevodin V.V. Computational foundations of linear algebra Moscow: Nauka, 1977.

French military officer and mathematician. The idea of this algorithm was published in 1924 by his fellow officer and, later, was used by Banachiewicz in 1938. In the Russian mathematical literature, the Cholesky decomposition is also known as the square-root method. The variance decomposition technique applied for each VAR model estimated separately for each currency pair data sampled from spot and future market. The result would be used to identify the response in endogenous variable caused by shock in each exogenous variable in the estimated VAR. Table 5.8 represents the output from variance decomposition analysis from estimated VAR of USD/INR spot rate and future rates. The result depicts that only 0.06% variance in USD/INR futures rate caused by shock in USD/INR spot rate which is insignificant. It also indicates that the 27% of variation in USD/INR spot rate caused by shock in USD/INR future rate signifying the impact of future rate on spot rate.

Table 5.8: Variance Decomposition of USD/INR spot rate and future rates.

Variance Decomposition of DUSDFUT:			
Period	**S.E.**	**DUSDFUT**	**DUSDSPOT**
1	0.280320	100.0000	0.000000
2	0.280423	99.94293	0.057066
3	0.281327	99.93462	0.065380
4	0.281327	99.93409	0.065914
5	0.281334	99.93401	0.065985
6	0.281334	99.93401	0.065989
7	0.281334	99.93401	0.065990
8	0.281334	99.93401	0.065990
9	0.281334	99.93401	0.065990
10	0.281334	99.93401	0.065990
Variance Decomposition of DUSDSPOT:			
Period	**S.E.**	**DUSDFUT**	**DUSDSPOT**
1	0.619856	26.69215	73.30785
2	0.620370	26.70954	73.29046
3	0.622602	27.20804	72.79196
4	0.622605	27.20809	72.79191
5	0.622623	27.21208	72.78792

6	0.622623	27.21208	72.78792
7	0.622623	27.21211	72.78789
8	0.622623	27.21211	72.78789
9	0.622623	27.21211	72.78789
10	0.622623	27.21211	72.78789
Cholesky Ordering: DUSDFUT DUSDSPOT			

Graph 5.1:

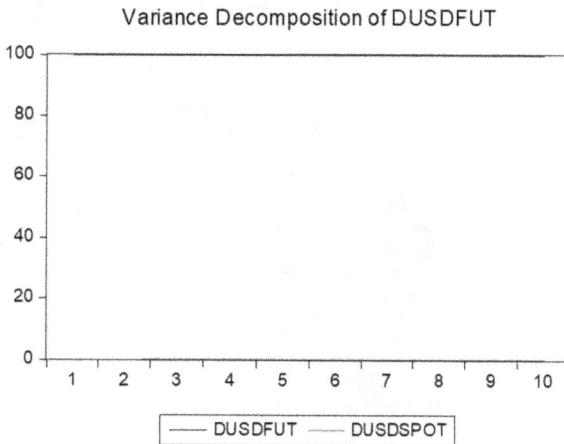

Variance Decomposition of DUSDFUT

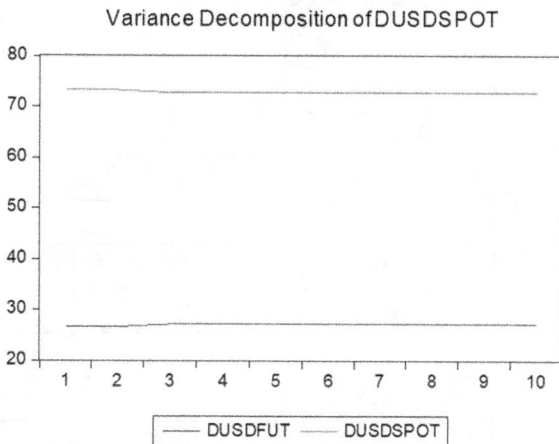

Variance Decomposition of DUSDSPOT

Table 5.9 represents the output from variance decomposition analysis from estimated VAR of JPY/INR spot rate and future rates. The result depicts that only 18% variance forecast error in JPY/INR futures rate caused by shock in JPY/INR spot rate over the period of 10 days which is relatively insignificant. It also indicates that the 55.8% of variation in JPY/INR spot rate caused by shock in JPY/INR future rate indicating a significant impact of the future rate on spot rate.

Table 5.9: Variance Decomposition of JPY/INR spot rate and future rates.

Variance Decomposition of DJPYFUT:			
Period	S.E.	DJPYFUT	DJPYSPOT
1	0.429883	100.0000	0.000000
2	0.473246	82.51928	17.48072
3	0.474305	82.17570	17.82430
4	0.475882	81.82200	18.17800
5	0.476191	81.71857	18.28143
6	0.476210	81.71740	18.28260
7	0.476214	81.71709	18.28291
8	0.476216	81.71668	18.28332
9	0.476216	81.71662	18.28338
10	0.476216	81.71662	18.28338
Variance Decomposition of DJPYSPOT:			
Period	S.E.	DJPYFUT	DJPYSPOT
1	0.014080	55.82651	44.17349
2	0.014083	55.83978	44.16022
3	0.014123	55.89901	44.10099
4	0.014123	55.89890	44.10110
5	0.014123	55.89936	44.10064
6	0.014123	55.89930	44.10070
7	0.014123	55.89929	44.10071
8	0.014123	55.89929	44.10071
9	0.014123	55.89929	44.10071
10	0.014123	55.89929	44.10071
Cholesky Ordering: DJPYFUT DJPYSPOT			

Graph 5.2:

Variance Decomposition of DJPYFUT

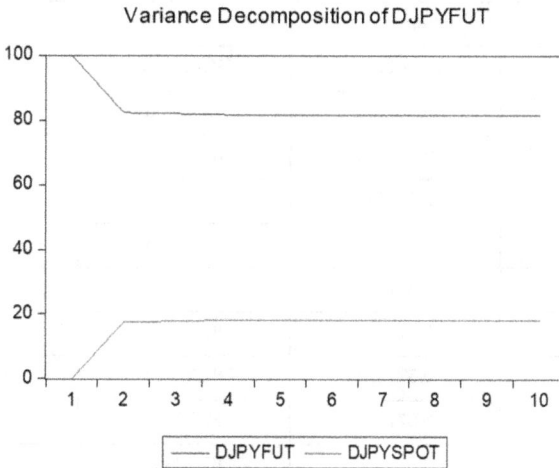

Variance Decomposition of DJPYSPOT

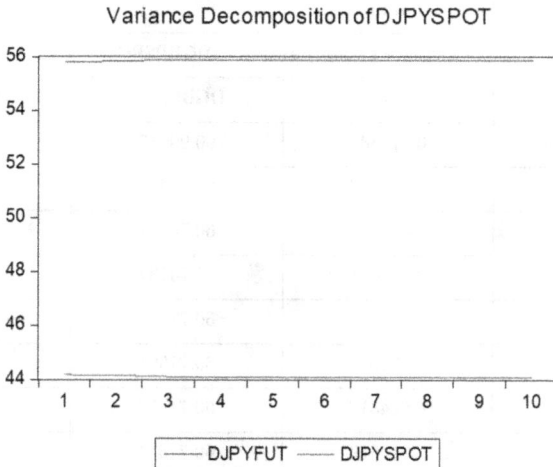

Table 5.10 represents the output from variance decomposition analysis from estimated VAR of GBP/INR spot rate and future rates. The result depicts that only 12% variance forecast error in GBP/INR futures rate caused by shock in GBP/INR spot rate which is found to be insignificant. It also indicates that the 61% of variation in GBP/INR spot rate caused by shock in GBP/INR future rate in a period of 10 days indicating a significant impact of the future rate on spot rate.

Table 5.10: Variance Decomposition of GBP/INR spot rate and future rates.

Period	S.E.	DGBPFUT	DGBPSPOT
Variance Decomposition of DGBPFUT:			
1	0.529465	100.0000	0.000000
2	0.567846	88.37070	11.62930
3	0.569556	87.90296	12.09704
4	0.571089	87.69876	12.30124
5	0.571450	87.58956	12.41044
6	0.571515	87.57805	12.42195
7	0.571519	87.57813	12.42187
8	0.571522	87.57737	12.42263
9	0.571523	87.57686	12.42314
10	0.571524	87.57681	12.42319
Variance Decomposition of DGBPSPOT:			
1	0.613384	60.99715	39.00285
2	0.621477	60.38337	39.61663
3	0.624650	60.74757	39.25243
4	0.624651	60.74737	39.25263
5	0.624765	60.72553	39.27447
6	0.624814	60.71591	39.28409
7	0.624817	60.71582	39.28418
8	0.624819	60.71574	39.28426
9	0.624819	60.71560	39.28440
10	0.624819	60.71558	39.28442
Cholesky Ordering: DGBPFUT DGBPSPOT			

Graph 5.3:

Variance Decomposition of DGBPFUT

Variance Decomposition of DGBPSPOT

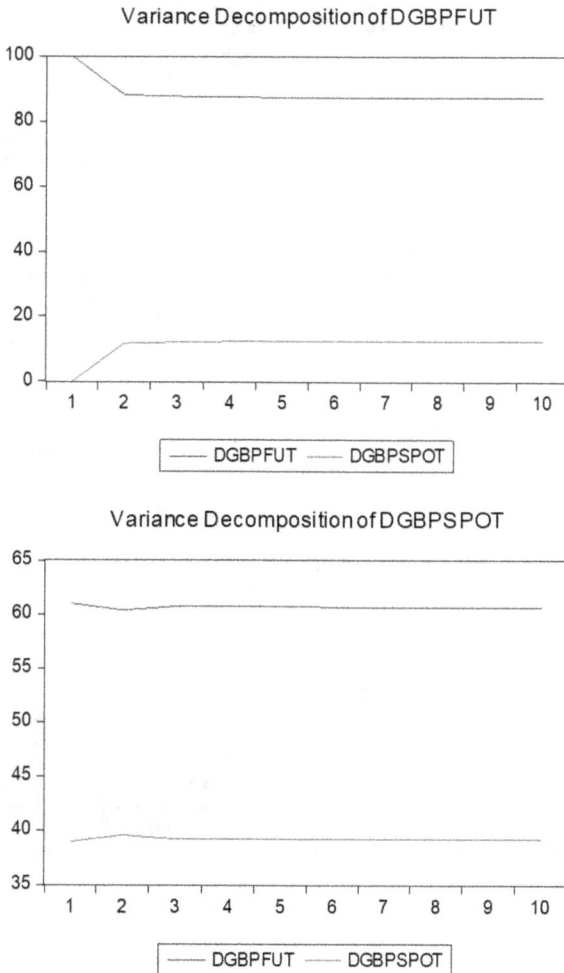

Table 5.11 represents the output from variance decomposition analysis from estimated VAR of EUR/INR spot rate and future rates. The result depicts that only 21% variance forecast error in EUR/INR futures rate caused by shock in EUR/INR spot rate over a period of 10 trading days which is insignificant. It also indicates that the 50% of variance forecast error in EUR/INR spot rate caused by shock in EUR/INR future rate in a period of 10 days indicating a significant impact of the future rate on spot rate.

Table 5.11: Variance Decomposition of EUR/INR spot rate and future rates.

Variance Decomposition of DEURFUT:			
Period	S.E.	DEURFUT	DEURSPOT
1	0.399747	100.0000	0.000000
2	0.450256	79.58620	20.41380
3	0.453078	78.63781	21.36219
4	0.454767	78.58596	21.41404
5	0.455053	78.50858	21.49142
6	0.455094	78.49857	21.50143
7	0.455101	78.49811	21.50189
8	0.455102	78.49817	21.50183
9	0.455102	78.49806	21.50194
10	0.455102	78.49803	21.50197
Variance Decomposition of DEURSPOT:			
Period	S.E.	DEURFUT	DEURSPOT
1	0.506717	50.37623	49.62377
2	0.510506	49.85129	50.14871
3	0.512942	50.32118	49.67882
4	0.512980	50.32859	49.67141
5	0.512994	50.32591	49.67409
6	0.513007	50.32344	49.67656
7	0.513008	50.32328	49.67672
8	0.513009	50.32334	49.67666
9	0.513009	50.32333	49.67667
10	0.513009	50.32333	49.67667
Cholesky Ordering: DEURFUT DEURSPOT			

Graph 5.4:

Variance Decomposition of DEURFUT

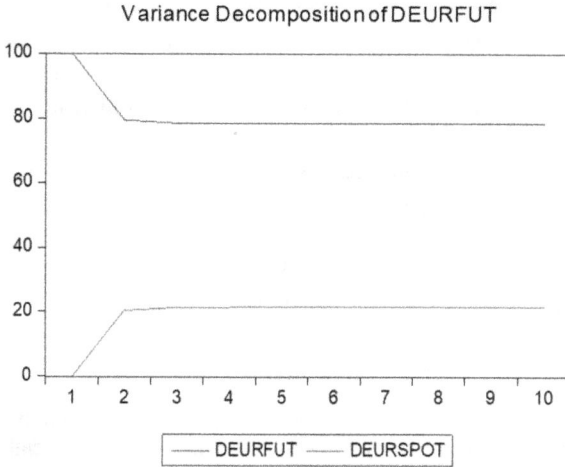

DEURFUT ——— DEURSPOT

Variance Decomposition of DEURSPOT

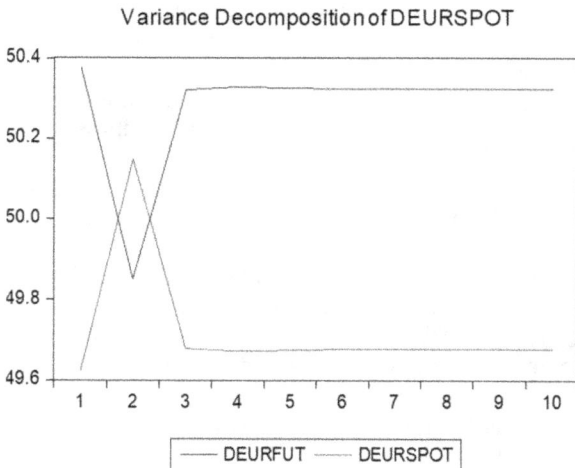

DEURFUT ——— DEURSPOT

Conclusion

The current study was aimed at examining the causal relationship between the NSE currency future rates and currency spot rates in order to identify the price discovery mechanism at NSE market. To study the causal relationship between the said markets, we have considered daily closing rates for NSE currency futures and currency spot rates for selected pairs of currencies, i.e. USD/INR, GBP/INR, JPY/INR and EURO/INR. Granger Causality Test is used for identifying the lead lag relationship between the currency spot and futures markets. From this study, we identified that the currency future rates lead spot rates for

USD/INR, GBR/INR and EURO/INR currency pairs. It is found that the spot rate for JPY/INR leads the future rate. It is also identified that the spot rate for USD/INR does not cause the changes in futures. It indicates that the market integration between spot and futures at NSE for currency pair USD/INR is strong compared to other selected currency pairs. From the variance decomposition test, we found that there is almost no impact of variance in USD/INR spot rate on future rate variance forecast errors. It implies that the causal relationship between for USD/INR spot and future rates is strong and mature compared to the measured causal relationships for remaining currency pairs. This study concludes that the price discovery process for currency pair USD/INR is better at NSE currency futures among the selected currency pairs.

References

Chan K. (1992). A further analysis of the lead-lag relationship between the cash market and stock index futures market. Review of Financial Studies, 5(1), 123–152.

De Boyrie, M.E., Pavlova, I. and Parhizgari, A.M. (2012), "Price discovery in currency markets: evidence from three emerging markets", International Journal of Economics and Finance, 4(12), 12-61.

Gonzalo, J. and Granger, C. (1995), "Estimation of common long-memory components in co integrated systems", Journal of Business and Economic Statistics, 13(1), 27-35.

Hans R. Stoll and Robert E. Whaley (1990). The Dynamics of Stock Index and Stock Index Futures Returns. *The Journal of Financial and Quantitative Analysis*, 25(4), 441-468.

Hasbrouck, J. (1995), "One security, many markets: determining the contributions to price discovery", Journal of Finance, 50(4), 1175-1199.

Ira G. Kawaller, Paul D. Koch and Timothy W. Koch (1987). The Temporal Price Relationship Between S&P 500 Futures and the S&P 500 Index. *The Journal of Finance*, 42(5), 1309-1329.

Lyons, Richard K. (2001). The Microstructure Approach to Exchange Rates. MIT Press, Cambridge, MA.

Srivastava, A. and Singh, M. (2015), "A study on pricing of currency futures in Indian currency market", International Journal of Research in Finance and Marketing, 5(6), 1-11.

Sehgal, S., Ahmad, W., & Deisting, F. (2018), Business Cycle and Financial cycle Interdependence, Journal of Quantitative Economics, 16(2), 337–362

Osler, C. L., Mende, A., & Menkhoff, L. (2011). Price discovery in currency markets. *Journal of International Money and Finance, 30*(8), 1696-1718.

Varuna Kharbanda and Archana Singh, (2017). Lead-lag relationship between futures and spot FX market in India. *International Journal of Managerial Finance*, 13(5), 560-577.

Voevodin V.V. Computational foundations of linear algebra Moscow: Nauka, 1977.

Chapter 6

Exchange Rate Risk in the Foreign Exchange Market: A Challenge on Corporate Profitability

Tejswini Basatry,
Research Scholar,
GITAM Institute of Management,
GITAM University, Visakhapatnam.

Prof. P. Sheela, MBA, Ph.D.,
Principal,
GITAM Institute of Management,
GITAM University, Visakhapatnam.

Introduction

The global foreign exchange market is the largest traded market in terms of trade volume, value, volatility and risk management. A foreign exchange system was considered to be a nascent market during the pre-liberalization period of India. The global market has seen many challenges after the breakup of the Bretton Woods administered fixed exchange rate system in 1971. Thus, a market determined exchange rate system was introduced in 1972. In the market based exchange rate determined system there was more fluctuation in the exchange rate around the global markets due to the increased effect of inflation, interest rate changes, oil price shock, political tension between Middle East countries, and Asian crises. Corporate at global level needs to go through these challenges in their cross broader trade activities as the means of impact on their profitability.

The Indian foreign exchange market had a similar situation to the global market until the pre-liberalization of the economy. The post-liberalization of the economy brought significant changes to the exchange rate system during the 1990s through monetary policy reforms. Until February 1992, the Reserve Bank of India (RBI) was deemed to be a decision maker in fixing the exchange rate in the foreign exchange market in India. But the external pressure over the call money rate pressure had thereafter brought a dual exchange rate system in March 1992, which was known as the Liberalized Exchange Rate Management System (LERMS). Then, the Unified Exchange rate was introduced in 1st March 1993. Even today, RBI fixes the reference rate for the exchange of foreign currencies at the end of the everyday.

The foreign exchange market faces the risks of transaction exposure, translation exposure, and operating exposure which seems to be part of the exchange rate determination. But these exchange rate movements had influenced over the corporate profitability. Firms with international business need to face the risks of exchange rate volatility over its import or export of raw materials, cash inflows and outflows of business transactions, which need to be managed at every level of its business operations. This paper highlights the problem of the exchange rate risk and its effect on corporate profitability as a major cause to be exchange rate scenario. The impact of foreign exchange rate movement on Indian IT (Information Technology) firms' revenue and its profitability is discussed in this paper. This will give a broad representation of exchange rate impact on corporate profitability and strengthening the growth scenario of future IT businesses in India.

Literature Review

Vashishtha and Kumar's (2010)[1] study 'how risk management is possible in an uncertain business scenario with the introduction of derivatives trading in India in June 2000?' SEBI permitted the derivatives segments of NSE and BSE and their clearing houses to commence trading and settlement of derivatives contracts. Since then the derivatives market has witnessed tremendous growth in India in terms of the number of traded contracts.

Dhandhayuthapani and Sarathkumar (2016)[2] study the investor's attitude towards derivatives market and awareness of the derivative market. The sample size for the study was 200 respondents based on convenience sampling. From the study, it was found that male respondents as compared to females invest in derivatives. It was also found that higher education plays a role in derivatives trading.

---

[1] Ashutosh Vashishtha, and Satish Kumar (2010), "Development of Financial Derivatives Market in India – A Case Study", International Research Journal of Finance and Economics, 37,15-29.
[2] Sarathkumar K and S. P. Dhandayuthapani (2016), Analytical Study on Indian Derivatives Market with Reference to Investors Attitude, International Journal for Innovative Research in Science & Technology, 2 (11).

Pradyumna Dash (2016)[3] observed that the crowding out effect of public investment on private investment has dampened during the post-liberalization period. The results also reveal that a "market friendly" incumbent and an increase in foreign direct investment dampen the magnitude of the crowding out effect of public investment. Formal tests were conducted to examine whether the crowding out effect was driven by political uncertainty and political business cycle channels, but no evidence for the same is found.

Sheng (2014)[4] investigates how managerial expertise—specifically, industry expertise—affects firm value through divestiture. Using CEOs' managerial experiences in industries throughout their careers as a measure of their industry expertise, the finding is consistent with CEOs who divest such divisions in order to refocus on those divisions in which they have specialized—that is, to achieve a better match between their expertise and their firms' retained assets. Firms that divest for a better CEO-firm match experience significant improvements in operating performance, as well as significant abnormal stock returns that persist for an average of three years following a divestiture.

Foreign exchange (FX) market

The FX market plays a significant role in global trade by determining the strength of an economy and its growth. The world moved into the transition of foreign exchange practices after Bretton Woods in 1944, and fixed to flexible exchange rate regime in 1972. During this period India has been following the global practices moving from peg exchange rate regime to a floating rate exchange system and is currently following a market based exchange system. The Indian exchange rate is being controlled by the Reserve Bank of India (RBI).

Global FX market comprises the spot market, the forward market, the future market, and the options in the derivatives market segment. In India during August 2008 the first foreign currency trading system was introduced against the US dollar, then the Euro, the British Pound Sterling and Japanese Yen in the National Stock Exchange of India (NSE), and then later in the Multi-Commodity Exchange of India for currency trading (MCX-SX), and Bombay Stock Exchange of India (BSE). Now there is the exclusive exchange started by BSE in the name of United Stock Exchange of India (USE).

---

[3] Pradyumna Dash (2001). The Impact of Public Investment on Private Investment: Evidence from India, *Vikalpa, The Journal for Decision Makers*, 41(4).

[4] Huang, Sheng, 2014. "Managerial Expertise, Corporate Decisions and Firm Value: Evidence from Corporate Refocusing," *Journal of Financial Intermediation, Elsevier*, 23(3), 348-375.

Foreign exchange rate risk

The risk of foreign exchange management is globally well understood by practitioners. The foreign exchange rate is unstable due to uncertainty over the interest rate, flow of capital from the foreign countries, changes in government policies, and its uncertainty over the taxation of foreign fund flow. In the past two decades, global foreign exchange rates volatility against most of the currencies have increased, especially with the globally traded currency of US dollar which turned out to be more volatile due to financial risks attributed to economic growth. During this period Indian currency did not leave behind the global problems as it needs to manage its exchange rate volatility risk against global currencies. Due to the effect of the origination of the global financial crisis in the United States, European slowdown, and high crude oil prices, the Indian foreign exchange rate depreciated the most reaching an all-time low of Rs.57.2165 against US dollar on 27th June 2012. The depreciation of the Indian currency value had a larger influence over the Indian corporate profitability for the firms depending upon the import of resources from the foreign country. It is by adding production cost and for an exporter is said to be favour as rupee depreciates. But the risk of a volatile exchange rate in the future market has a negative impact on the fixing of the exchange rate in the spot market, and the covering of the same in the futures market by the hedgers.

Historical foreign exchange rate

The historical trend of foreign exchange rate in India shows the continuous depreciation of Indian rupee against the US dollar and other major currencies. The foreign exchange rate of Indian currency against the US dollar shows that the exchange rate was only Rs.7.66 Vs 1US $ during 1973. The economic scenario which had brought a greater fall in the rupee value is listed on Table 6.1. The table shows year wise historical changes in the Indian foreign exchange rate. The average exchange rate of Indian rupee standards was at Rs.52.68 for the period ending March 2012, having depreciated the most against US dollar of Rs.53.90 Vs 1US $ as on 23rd September 2012. This one-sided movement on exchange rate boosted the domestic firms which are based on export-oriented businesses, and brought pain for the importing firms which are dependent on import of raw material, or finished goods from a foreign country.

Table 6.1: Foreign Exchange Rate of Indian Rupee (INR) Vs US Dollar ($).

Year	INR/USD	Year	INR/USD	Year	INR/USD
1973	7.66	1988	13.91	2003	46.60
1974	8.03	1989	16.21	2004	45.28
1975	8.41	1990	17.50	2005	44.01
1976	8.97	1991	22.72	2006	45.17
1977	8.77	1992	28.14	2007	41.20
1978	8.20	1993	31.26	2008	43.41
1979	8.16	1994	31.39	2009	48.32
1980	7.89	1995	32.43	2010	45.65
1981	8.68	1996	35.52	2011	46.61
1982	9.48	1997	36.36	2012	53.90
1983	10.11	1998	41.33	2013	53.77
1984	11.36	1999	43.12	2014	60.31
1985	12.34	2000	45.00	2015	63.60
1986	12.60	2001	47.23	2016	66.34
1987	12.95	2002	48.62	2017	65.055

Source: http://www.forecast-chart.com/usd-indian rupee.html

The foreign exchange rate of Indian currency shows historical depreciation of exchange value not only with the US dollar but also against the British Pound Sterling, the Euro, and the Japanese Yen. The high volatile movement of these exchange rates has mostly influenced the corporate earnings and economic growth potential to a larger extent. This high risk involvement in the exchange of foreign currencies, even from the early period of the exchange system, had a direct impact on corporate profitability. In the past 20 years, after the liberalization of the economy, Indian currency have depreciated most comparatively against all the global currencies.

During 1990-91 the Indian economy faced foreign exchange crisis, which forced the Indian economy to be liberalized. During the same period, the foreign exchange rate of India depreciated most between the period of 1988 to 1993. Later the 1997 Asian financial crisis, which also coincided with Dot-com bubble in 1995-2000 peaking out after rapid growth in economic activities, had an impact on the foreign currency exchange rate. In the 2008 housing bubble which started in the US have spread into Europe and created financial instability and liquidity problems against the exchange of rupee against the US dollar, the rupee depreciated from 43.41 to 48.32 in 2008-2009.

Basic framework of risk management

Risk management is basically practiced to minimize the loss of the notional loss of the currency fluctuations in the international market. For this, a validated framework is adopted by many firms based on the model developed for understanding and hedging the risk exposure. It starts with the forecast of the business value, and trend of the exchange rate risk analysis. Based on this finding, benchmarking is done to cover-up the cost or profitability of the hedging and the exposure of the business value. Validation and review of the profitability are finally done. The basics of the risk management technique is to solve the systematic risk involved in the exchange market.

Corporate Risk Management

For corporate, managing foreign exchange risk in a volatile market is a great job. Corporate needs to anticipate the exchange rate risk in order to offset market loss in the foreign exchange market. The instruments used for managing foreign exchange rate risk is done through forward contract, Over The Counter (OTC) Exchange rate system, future contract, swap, and options by hedging the value of trade in the foreign exchange market. Many firms try to hedge their business transactions to minimize the loss, which could be gained through currency future in the foreign exchange market. The hedging opportunity exists for the firms to take up the position either in the long or short side, based on the market trend. The hedging instruments offer the benefit of managing the risk, if the traders do not know the direction of the market movement. In the case of information technology firms, the revenue flow comes through the foreign currencies. These firms are directly influenced by the exchange rate fluctuations. Taking the case of Infosys, its primary revenue comes as US dollar, Euro or the Pound. Infosys manages its revenue by hedging in the foreign currency market against the US dollar or Euro.

Impact on corporate profitability

The impact of foreign exchange rate volatility could influence the economic performance and corporate earnings directly. The corporate earnings of the IT (Information Technology) industry depend on the exchange rate system compared with the agreed contract price and date of bill generation for the service delivered. But the question is that, does the same exchange rate exist as that of the agreed contact date. If it does not exist as that of agreed price; this might benefit either person based on the contract rate and exchange rate. The most benefited industry might be large IT firms and the small size firms who could not bear this problem initially. Even the large-scale IT firms like Infosys face exchange rate volatility problems as their revenue comes from the US dollar, the United Kingdom Pound Sterling, the Euro and the Australian dollar, whereas the firms' expenses are met through the Indian rupees. The exchange rate between the rupee and the foreign currency like the US dollar has a major impact on the profit margin of the firm substantially. The key factors affecting the exchange rate fluctuations are mainly due to:

- The country in which the firm operates its business

- Size and time of the project operation during the economic cycle

- Pricing policy of the competitors and a firm position Economic strength of the operating nation and vice-versa

- Inflation pressure over salary payment to the employees

- Political stability of the nation is the firm that operates Government control over the exchange rate system Unanticipated move of the economic developments through political pressures

Conclusion

The exchange rate fluctuations could have major implications on the corporate profits. It is an attempt to know the impact of exchange rates which could impact over the corporate profitability. Although the majority of the firms could not avoid the volatility of the exchange rate scenario, this could be managed through proper hedging system adopted by the firm systematically. It is a fine example of how most of the IT firms operate across the globe, but the differences in currency rate are part of their earnings. All being hedged systematically and some may lead to noticeable market loss which can be a notional loss in the books of the accounts. In reality, exchange rate volatility could add pressure to corporate profits. So it is better to go with the circumstances and follow the global rule to get profit out the differences and volatility in the foreign exchange market. Thus, it is concluded that the corporate needs to manage their foreign revenues by hedging their positions in the foreign currency futures market. This strategy could improve corporate profitability by minimizing the exchange rate risk in the foreign exchange market.

References

Ashutosh V & S. Kumar (2010), "Development of Financial Derivatives Market in India – A Case Study", *International Research Journal of Finance and Economics*, 37,15-29.

Huang, S (2014), "Managerial expertise, corporate decisions and firm value: Evidence from corporate refocusing," *Journal of Financial Intermediation*, Elsevier, 23(3), 348-375.

Pradyumna, D (2016), "The Impact of Public Investment on Private Investment: Evidence from India", *Vikalpa, The Journal for Decision Makers*, 41(4).

Sarathkumar K & S. P. Dhandayuthapani (2016), "Analytical Study on Indian Derivatives Market with Reference to Investors Attitude", *International Journal for Innovative Research in Science & Technology*, 2 (11).

Chapter 7

Forex Exchange Management and Challenges in Current Global Economic Environment

Dr. Shamshuddin Shaik,
Assistant Professor, GITAM University.
Mobile No.: +91-8019716116
Email: shamshuddin1234@gmail.com

Dr. Shaik Khadar Baba,
Andhra University.
Mobile No.: +91-9989570027
Email: skkbaba@yahoo.com

Dr. Haniefuddin Shaik,
Director NISTV.
Email: haniefuddin@rediffmail.com

Introduction

The foreign exchange market commonly referred to as Forex or FX, is the largest financial market where currencies are bought, sold and exchanged one for another. Unlike, for example, stocks market that have no centralized exchange and transactions are performed over-the-counter, that is, participants trade with one another through a worldwide network of banks, brokers and other financial institutions. As the global market Forex is opened for 24 hours a day and 5 days a week, i.e. Monday to Friday (Rekha and Mary, 2017).[1]

The major financial centers are based across almost every time zone in London, New York, Tokyo, Zurich, Frankfurt, Hong Kong, Singapore, Paris and Sydney. Depending on the exchange active during a specific time, one can distinguish between three trading sessions: Asian, European and American. Foreign exchange currencies are quoted against one another in pairs

---

[1] Rekha, A. V. S., & Mary, S. (2017). A Study of Foreign Exchange Rate Volatility on Nifty. *Imperial Journal of Interdisciplinary Research*, 3(2).

and the price indicates how much of quote currency is required to buy or sell one unit of base currency.

Important factors affecting forex market

According to Goyal (2016), "the exchange rate is one of the most important determinants of a country's relative level of economic health. It plays a vital role in trade, which is critical to most free market economies."[2] But exchange rates matter on a smaller scale too. They even impact the real return of an investor's portfolio.

Differentials in Inflation

As a general rule, a country with a consistently lower inflation rate exhibits a rising currency value, as its purchasing power increases relative to other currencies. Those countries with higher inflation typically see depreciation in their currency's value in relation to the currencies of their trading partners.

Differentials in Interest Rates

By manipulating interest rates, central banks exert influence over both inflation and exchange rates. Higher interest rates offer lenders a higher return relative to other countries. (Hernandez et al., 2018)[3]. The impact of higher interest rates is mitigated, however, if a country's inflation is much higher than other countries, or if additional factors serve to drive their currency value down. The opposite relationship exists for decreasing interest rates.

Current-Account Deficits

The current account is the balance of trade between a country and its trading partners, reflecting all payments between countries for goods, services, interest and dividends. A deficit in the current account shows a country is importing goods and services more than it is exporting them. The country will then typically borrow capital from foreign sources to make up the defi-

[2] Goyal, A. (2016), "Foreign exchange markets, intervention, and exchange rate regimes", in Roy, M. and Roy, S.S. (Eds), International Trade and International Finance, Springer, New Delhi, pp. 469-492.

[3] Hernandez-Aguila, A., Garcia-Valdez, M., & Castillo, O. (2018). Money Management for a Foreign Exchange Trading Strategy Using a Fuzzy Inference System. In *Fuzzy Logic Augmentation of Neural and Optimization Algorithms: Theoretical Aspects and Real Applications*, pp. 275-286.

cit, causing its currency to depreciate relative to its trading partner (Singh and Jain, 2018).[4]

Public Debt

Countries will engage in large-scale deficit financing to pay for public sector projects using governmental funding. While such activity stimulates the domestic economy, nations with large public deficits and debts are less attractive to foreign investors. A large debt encourages more inflation, and higher inflation translates into lower currency value.

Terms of Trade

Are a country's terms of trade a ratio comparing export prices to import prices? If the price of a country's exports rises by a greater rate than that of its imports, its terms of trade have favorably improved, which tends to show currency appreciation. However, if the price of a country's imports rises more than the rate of exports, their currency's value will be decreased in relation to trading partners.

Political Stability and Economic Performance

Foreign investors inevitably seek out stable countries with strong economic performance in which to invest their capital. Political turmoil, for example, can cause a loss of confidence in a currency, and a movement of capital to the currencies of more stable countries.

Another detrimental factor in price setting are orders from Forex market participants that are quite diverse in the volume they generate and influence they have. Governments and central banks such as the European Central Bank, the Bank of England, and the Federal Reserve of the US operate with the largest volumes and have the most influence on exchange rates. Central banks try to control inflation, money supply, interest rates and are in charge of supervising commercial banking systems. They can use foreign exchange reserves to intervene in the market to stabilize currency rates or achieve a specific economic goal. Foremost banks and bank associations that form so-called interbank market, through which they transact with each other and determine the currency price individual traders observe in the trading platform.

---

[4] Singh, U. P., & Jain, S. (2018). Optimization of neural network for nonlinear discrete time system using modified quaternion firefly algorithm: case study of Indian currency exchange rate prediction. Soft Computing, 22(8), 2667-2681.

The prime motive of the foreign exchange policy is to manage imports and exports and secondly to restrict the unofficial influx of foreign currencies inside the country through the Reserve Bank of India. The exchange rate policy is guided by the following objectives:

    i.   to eliminate lumpy demand and supply in the foreign exchange market without reference to any target of exchange rate;

    ii.   to prevent speculative attack; and

    iii.   to maintain an adequate amount of reserves.

Alternative exchange rate regime:

Countries have three basic choices in determining the monetary linkage between their economy and the rest of the world, assuming that they maintain a currency of their own. Any country can let their currency float freely in the exchange markets against all other currencies; they can fix the price of their currency against a specific foreign currency or a basket of foreign currencies; or they can pursue intermediate approaches, letting rates float to some extent but intervening to limit those fluctuations either ad hoc or pursuant to some pre-determined parameters.

An exchange-rate regime is the way an authority manages its currency in relation to other currencies and the foreign exchange market. Between the two limits of fixed and freely floating exchange regimes, there can be other types of regimes (Kawaller et al., 1987).[5] In their operational objective, it is closely related to monetary policy of the country with both depending on common factors of influence and impact. The exchange rate regime has a big impact on world trade and financial flows. The volume of such transactions and the speed at which they are growing makes the exchange rate regime a central piece of any national economic policy framework.

The Reserve Bank of India's selective control in the Forex market has been unable to control the free fall in the value of rupee in recent years. This raises a fundamental question as to whether the RBI should consider alternative exchange rate policy options. Specifically, would a move towards a completely fixed or floating exchange rate regime offer immediate help to the country?

---

[5] Kawaller I.G., Koch P.D., & Koch T.W. (1987). The Temporal Price Relationship between S&P 500 futures and the S&P 500 index. *The Journal of Finance*, 42(5), 1309–1329.

Fixed (pegged) Exchange Rate	Adjustable Peg	Crawling Peg	Managed Float	Wider Band System	Freely Floating Exchange Rates
↓	↑	↑	↑	↑	↓
A					B

Types of Exchange Rate Regime

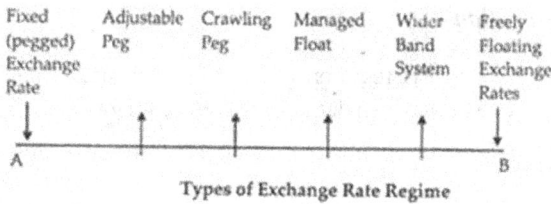

As one moves from point A on the left to point B on the right, both the frequency of intervention by domestic monetary authorities and required level of international reserves tend to be lower.

Under a pure fixed-exchange-rate regime (point A), authorities intervene so that the value of the domestic currency vis-à-vis the currency of another country, say the US Dollar, is maintained at a constant rate (Bhadra, 2018).[6] Under a freely floating exchange-rate regime, authorities do not intervene in the market for foreign exchange, and there is minimal need for international reserves.

Exchange Rate System in India

India was among the original members of the IMF when it began in 1946. As such, India was obliged to adopt the Bretton Woods system of exchange rate determination. This system is known as the par value system of pegged exchange rate system. Under this system, each member country of the IMF was required to define the value of its currency in terms of gold or the US dollar and maintain (or peg) the market value of its currency within ± percent of the defined (par) value.

Intervention by RBI

The current exchange rate regime, introduced in 1993, the RBI has been, actively intervening in the foreign exchange market with the objective of maintaining the real effective exchange rate (REER) stable.

The RBI uses two types of intervention in this regard

Direct Intervention

It refers to purchases and sales in international currency, i.e. US dollars and euro both on the spot and also in forward markets.

---

[6] Bhadra, S. (2018). Sector-wise Differential Growth Rate of Indian Economy and the Threat of Inflation. *Asian Journal of Research in Social Sciences and Humanities*, 8(4), 76-84.

Indirect Intervention

It refers to the use of reserve requirements and interest rate flexibility to smoothen temporary mismatches between demand and supply of foreign currency.

The general problem of the mismatch between the constraints of the anchor and the needs of the economy can take three forms:

1) Loss of monetary independence,

2) Loss of automatic adjustment to export shocks, and

3) Extraneous volatility.

The problem of the balance of payments is the macro issue of the foreign exchange rate. The balance of payments is influenced by the foreign exchange rate. The exchange rate is the value of a national currency in terms of a foreign currency (Dash et al., 2008).[7]

The exchange rate is a price, and its determination can be explained through the demand for and supply of foreign exchange. In the long-run, the foreign exchange rate between the two currencies is determined by the purchasing powers of the two currencies in the domestic economies. In the short-run, the demand for imports and exports of goods and services, the magnitude of capital flows between the countries affects demand for and supply of foreign exchange and thereby determine the exchange rate between the currencies.

Foreign Exchange Rate, Balance of Payments and Capital Inflows and Outflows

Changes in the foreign exchange rate have an important effect on the balance of payments of a country. When there is depreciation or devaluation in the currency of a country, its exports become cheaper and imports costlier than before.

This causes exports to increase and imports to decrease causing a reduction in the deficit in the balance of payments. Thus, in order to check the increase in the deficit in the balance of payments and to restore equilibrium in it, devaluation or depreciation of the domestic currency against foreign currencies is often undertaken.

Besides, the foreign exchange inflows in various forms such as those resulting from rising exports, portfolio investment by FIIs (Foreign Institutional

---

[7] Dash, Mihir and Kodagi, Mahesh and B. Y., Vivekanand and Babu, Narendra, (2008). An Empirical Study of Forex Risk Management Strategies. *Indian Journal of Finance*, II (8).

Investors), foreign direct investment (FDI) not only causes appreciation of exchange rate of the domestic currency.

Depreciation of currency is considered to be desirable as it boosts exports and reduces imports. But a sharp depreciation of the rupee in the present macroeconomic situation has had a serious consequence. Not only will it make imports costlier and fuel another round of inflation, but it will also restrain the RBI from pushing through the cuts in repo rate and cash reserve ratio urgently needed for kick-starting investments and boosting growth Breaking out of this policy log-jam requires the government to curtail current account deficit (CAD).

Volatility of exchange rates may distort resource allocation.

Monetary policy needs to be framed in terms of nominal anchors different from exchange rates.

Inflation bias may be large.

Lack of transparency of RBI:

If the band is narrow, the system can be prone to speculative attacks. Selecting the band is difficult. Allowing for the possibility of the realignment of the bands and central parity weaken the credibility.

A backward-looking can introduce inflationary inertia, whereas a forward-looking can produce overvaluation and give rise to speculative pressures.

Tests to ascertain the validity of exchange rate targeting:

To test for the validity of the "exchange-rate targeting" by the RBI we carried out two simple exercises. The first one calculated a neutral real effective exchange rate (REER) from the 36-country REER and the deviation from such. The second one calculated the deviations of the nominal exchange rate from a PPP value using the country REER. In both the cases, it can be found a strong correlation between the overvaluation of the REER and disturbances in the foreign exchange market and the subsequent RBI policy actions to nudge it towards the REER neutral level.

RBI Intervention in The Foreign Exchange Market

RBI's intervention in the currency markets to support the Indian currency, including a massive sell-off of dollars.

Direct Intervention

In case of any currency movement, a country's central bank can directly intervene to either push the currency up, as India has been doing or to keep it artificially low, as the Chinese central bank does. To push up a currency, a central bank can sell dollars, which is the global reserve currency, or the currency against which all others are measured. When it needs to keep its currency lower, it can buy dollars, as the Chinese do, to the point where they are the largest holders of dollar-backed US Treasury paper.

Indirect Intervention

A central bank can also intervene indirectly by regulatory action. The banking regulator has relaxed caps on the interest rates for foreign currency non-resident deposits (FCNR) in the hope that this will attract depositors to put more dollars into such accounts. It has also allowed banks to self-regulate export credit limits.

The rupee's gains have come as the central bank has stepped up its rhetoric on inflation, with investors seeing the authority as turning increasingly hawkish. The forwards intervention strategy will cause importers' hedging to fall, while exporters will be incentivized to hedge. RBI's intervention through the forwards market will keep foreign-exchange swap rates at elevated levels.

At the same time, the high foreign exchange volatility raised the concern about the risk of overshooting which could weigh negatively on investment and growth in the affected economies. Volatility in exchange rate refers to the amount of uncertainty or risk involved with the size of changes in a currency's exchange rate. Volatility in the rupee-dollar exchange rates during various episodes of heightened volatility in the Forex market in the past two decades can be computed using standard deviations of daily Forex market returns, which have been annualized.

The official intervention in the foreign exchange market in the form of buying and selling foreign currency assets can be of two types: sterilized intervention and no sterilized intervention. Official intervention is sterilized if the authority acts to offset the impact of intervention on the domestic monetary base (Johansen and Juselius, 1990).[8]

For instance, the domestic monetary base tends to increase in response to the net official purchase of foreign exchange from the market. Such expansion in money supply can be offset by conducting an open market sale of securities or by resorting to other monetary instruments that would reduce the monetary base.

---

[8] Johansen S. and Juselius K. (1990). Maximum likelihood estimation and inference on co-integration – with applications to the demand for money. *Oxford Bulletin of Economics and Statistics*, 52, 169–210.

On the contrary, non-sterilized intervention occurs when the authority buys foreign exchange against its own currency without taking offsetting action. Thus, non-sterilized intervention affects domestic money supply which, in turn, affects the exchange rate. However, to what extent exchange rate responses to non-sterilized intervention depends upon the extent to which change (Osler et al., 2011)[9]in money supply affects the exchange rate. A better understanding of the issue on intervention work can be found from the various theories that explain the transmission mechanism between intervention and exchange rate variations. Broadly speaking, the official purchase or sale of foreign exchange affects the exchange rate through three different channels: (i) portfolio channel; (ii) signaling channel or expectation channel; and (iii) Noise trading channel.

Conclusion

Operating in a globalized environment is being answerable to the different countries which have different political environments as well as trade procedures. In addition, the credit conditions may be totally different from what they are domestically. Anticipating day-to-day financial management challenges when operating internationally and devising ways to maintain healthy equilibrium within this economic framework ensure your business' continued growth and survival. In a globalized economy, the cash that goes in and out of the various countries is subject to fluctuations in exchange rates. This creates uncertainty for financial managers when it comes to the value of the home currency in relation to foreign currencies. Continuous fluctuations in the foreign exchange market could mean slow business for global organizations. If you need part of your financing for projects in emerging economies where you conduct your business, fluctuating exchange rates can subject you to higher interest rates. You have to monitor the foreign exchange market closely for suitable rates that benefit your organization.

References

Bhadra, S. (2018). Sector Wise Differential Growth Rate of Indian Economy and the Threat of Inflation. Asian Journal of Research in Social Sciences and Humanities, 8(4), 76-84.

Dash, Mihir and Kodagi, Mahesh and B. Y., Vivekanand and Babu, Narendra, (2008) An Empirical Study of Forex Risk Management Strategies. *Indian Journal of Finance*, II (8).

---

[9] Osler, C. L., Mende, A., & Menkhoff, L. (2011). Price discovery in Currency Markets. *Journal of International Money and Finance, 30*(8), 1696-1718.

Goyal, A. (2016), "Foreign exchange markets, intervention, and exchange rate regimes", in Roy, M. and Roy, S.S. (Eds), International Trade and International Finance, Springer, New Delhi, pp. 469-492.

Hernandez-Aguila, A., Garcia-Valdez, M., & Castillo, O. (2018). Money Management for a Foreign Exchange Trading Strategy Using a Fuzzy Inference System. In *Fuzzy Logic Augmentation of Neural and Optimization Algorithms: Theoretical Aspects and Real Applications*, pp. 275-286.

Johansen S. and Juselius K. (1990). Maximum likelihood estimation and inference on co integration – with applications to the demand for money. *Oxford Bulletin of Economics and Statistics*, 52, 169–210.

Kawaller I.G., Koch P.D., & Koch T.W. (1987). The temporal price relationship between S&P 500 futures and the S&P 500 index. The Journal of Finance, 42(5), 1309–1329.

Osler, C. L., Mende, A., & Menkhoff, L. (2011). Price discovery in currency markets. *Journal of International Money and Finance, 30*(8), 1696-1718.[1].
Rekha, A. V. S., & Mary, S. (2017). A Study of Foreign Exchange Rate Volatility on Nifty. *Imperial Journal of Interdisciplinary Research, 3*(2).

Singh, U. P., & Jain, S. (2018). Optimization of neural network for nonlinear discrete time system using modified quaternion firefly algorithm: case study of Indian currency exchange rate prediction. Soft Computing, 22(8), 2667-2681.

Chapter 8

Assessment of Operational Risk Management - Global vs Local Banking Sector

Dr.G.V.Satya Sekhar,
Associate Professor,
GITAM (Deemed to be University),
Visakhapatnam.

Dr.N.R.Mohan Prakash,
Assistant Professor,
GITAM (Deemed to be University),
Visakhapatnam.

Introduction

The assessment of operational risk management is becoming vital on account of organizational, infrastructure, business environment, or technological changes. These changes materialized in the development of technology, the increase of attention to the transparency, the increase of operations for the natural person and small economic agents, deregulation, the incompatibility of systems, globalization and the increased use of the external sources. All these influences a healthy management of the operational risk and the inclusion in the internal process of a commercial bank.

The financial institutions consider that this risk appears in the departments called "Operations" and are concretized into potential losses generated by errors and controls, systems and processes omissions. But there are some institutions that consider the operational risk as the risk that do not harmonize with the credit or market risks and which incorporates all the risks.

Operational risks can affect the institution solvency and can generate a wrong approach from the consumers and also a lack of trust for the banking market.

In this article, special attention is given to identify the effects of operational risk from external sources, because improper information can expose the financial institution to very important operational risks.

What is operational risk?

The most used operational risk examples involve: system breakdowns or system errors; transactions process or control of errors; the activity stop; internal or external criminal acts; security disrespect or staff risks; improper control at all levels; the inexistence of the responsibility and of regulations for an integrated system, which can record wrongly data for a long period of time. Operational risk appears at different levels, as: personal level: human error, inexperience, fraud (they are recorded as destructions, false information or hide of information); procedures level: improper procedures and control regulations in order to create the reports for the national institutions responsible with the operational risk, to monitor and to take a decision; technique level: the implementation or the absence of the inadequate instruments used to measure the operational risk; technological level: system errors.

Operational risk management programs were made to understand the institutional risks, because of the operational risk exposure and the events produced during the last years. The new frame of the operational risk management presents five development stages that have a purpose and the priority identification. Also, this frame has a strong connection with the integration processes, the instruments and strategies of reduction this type of risk.

According to the Basel II Agreement, operational loss represents the loss resulted from an event of operational loss. This loss includes all the expenses related to this event, excepting opportunity costs, known income and the cost related to risk management and increased control operation, used to prevent future operational losses.

Literature Review

The specialized literature presents the opinions of more authors regarding the operational risk area. The PNC Financial Services Group recommended a more concise definition for the operational risk, a definition that should be based more on direct losses and which excludes categorically the business risk, the strategic risk and the reputational risk: "the operational risk is the risk of the income direct loss, which results from internal events connected to inadequate personal, important errors or illegal behavior because of the errors or the systems and processes inadequate, or from external events where the risks are not cover by the credit, market or interest rate risk". Operational risk, as one of the key risks that banks face, is reflected in the Basel II framework, which expects banks to identify measures and to manage this risk. Moreover, the Basel Committee requires banks to hold capital against operational risk. Thus, operational risk can be interpreted as a vulnerability of the financial institution that can be reduced or eliminated through increased control.

Ghosh (2010)[1] states that reputation risk can be quantified. In her study, she explained this with a recent example of the Swiss bank UBS's loss of $2.3 bn. This loss was a result of unauthorized trading. Recently, operation fraud at Societe Generale, -Web Serve survey[2] reveals that 68 percent of respondents said that data breaches happen when employees take confidential data with them when leaving a company. However, 63 percent of respondents opined that the ultimate responsibility of data loss should lie with the board of the organization.

Fheili (2007)[3] analyzed the factors that influence a firm's (bank) staff-related operational risk and provides some risk-mitigation strategies. In particular, he focuses on determinants that influence the retention of core employees, since new employees typically still have to build relevant skills and knowledge and hence are more likely to make mistakes (to deal with the loyal customers of the bank). Moreover, he argues that any delay in providing new employees with guidance, equipment and training as well as a lack of autonomy, recognition, lack of an interesting work environment and opportunities for growth lead to unintended staff turnover. A strategy for retention, he suggests that clarifying what the employee finds rewarding, recognizing engaged and motivated employees and establishing the firm's internal compensation and individual treatment mechanisms.

Breden (2008)[4] discusses the effectiveness of key risk indicators in monitoring the risk environment of financial institutions and suggests some activities (such as a bank's overseas payment business) that may be connected with higher risk and therefore may cause higher losses. He argues those activities that bear higher risk exposure should be identified and incorporated as elements when creating risk indicators, suggesting, for instance, the volume of errors and unreconciled items as a frequent indicator of risk. Moreover, he argues that alerts provided by risk indicators (e.g., the number and volume of payments exceeding an ex-ante specified monetary figure) enable the bank to address the problem quicker and should be communicated to all corresponding parties.

---

[1] Sowmya Kanthi Gosh, Measures of reputation risk, Dec 8th 2011, Financial Express.
[2] Web Serve survey results published in 'Xotoday', date April 14th, 2010.
[3] Fheili, M.I. Employee turnover: An HR risk with firm-specific context. J. Oper. Risk 2007, 2, 69–84.
[4] Breden, D (2008). Monitoring the Operational Risk Environment Effectively. *Journal of Risk Management in Financial Institutions*, 1, 156–164.

Peccia (2003)[5] argues that modeling operational risk has become important in relation to analyze the operational risk of a particular bank because the environment in which banks operate has changed dramatically. Rao and Dev (2006)[6] stated that the 'Advanced Measurement Approach' is about managing operational risk and calculating regulatory capital. Bolton and Berkey (2005)[7] stated that the Advanced Measurement Approach provides an excellent outline for designing an operational risk management framework that can provide tangible benefits and does not get distracted by the challenges of operational risk modeling.

As a basis, Jack Copeland[8] has six principles which are given as:

1. Hazard identification – using strict traditional procedures which analyze more and more hazards with one of the following basic instruments: operations analysis or financial flow diagram, the preliminary hazard analysis, scenarios, logic diagrams, change of analysis, cause-effect.

2. Risk evaluation – it is made in order to determine the fundamental causes and to establish the risk levels to use the risk evaluation matrix in order to make the risk a priority, from the biggest to the smallest.

3. The analysis of the risk control measures – it is made in order to develop the management of each type of risk. A good evaluation is made only if the control options are explored at macro level and the hazard control is identified.

4. The control decisions - they must be taken by the proper person and at the proper time on the basis of the proper support and data, but knowing the financial authority for taking decisions, the limits and the risks must be considered.

---

[5] Peccia, A (2003). Using Operational Risk Models to Manage Operational Risk. In C. Alexander (Ed.), *Operational Risk: Regulation, Analysis and Management*, London: Prentice Hall-Financial Times.

[6] Rao, V. and Dev, A (2006). Operational Risk: Some Issues in Basel II AMA Implementation in US Financial Institutions. In E. Davis (Ed.), *The Advanced Measurement Approach to Operational Risk*, London: Risk Books.

[7] Bolton, N. and Berkey, J. (2005). Aligning Basel II Operational Risk and Sarbanes- Oxley 404 Projects. In E. Davis (Ed.), *Operational Risk: Practical Approaches to Implementation*. London: Risk Books.

[8] Jack Copeland," *Operational Risk Management (ORM)"* - WR-ALC / SES.

5. The risk control implementation supposes the implementation of the developed strategies. These strategies define the individual responsibilities, the accountancy and the involvement of each person.

6. The surveillance and monitoring – suppose a systematic evaluation of the mission-oriented on performance results of the operational risk management determined in real time and on valid data for future applications. To comply with the conditions of a good evaluation, there should be a direct risk measure and a feedback mechanism.

Taking into consideration the losses suffered in the last years, the financial institutions changed the operational risk management. So, they established as main objectives: a higher capital profitability, a better capital allocation, the avoidance of the unanticipated losses, the avoidance of a big number of losses of small value, the improvement of the operational efficiency; greater attention to the operational risk during the banking management process; the increase of the services quality for the clients; efficient information and human resources management.

Therefore, a financial institution must have:

i. A restrictive operational risk management process, data and exchange systems and also systems to measure the risk and to determine the capital need for this risk;

ii. A management functions for the operational risk. This function has to be independent of the business line management, but responsible for the design, implementation and data and evaluation systems surveillance and quantification;

iii. A process to identify, measure, monitor and administrate products, activities, processes and systems.

Keeping in mind that operational risk is not only a simple regulatory necessity but also an investment through the optimal allocation of the economic capital by using Risk Adjusted Return on Capital. This index represents a correct evaluation of the risk costs and a better knowledge of the clients and their behavior and of the organization and its processes.

To determine the operational risk level, the financial institution has to accomplish some general demands:

- the formal frame for the activity management has to be strict,

- has to have an organizational structure very clear, with precise, transparent and coherent responsibilities;

- has to have an efficient process of identification, administration, monitoring and report of risk;

- has to have a proper internal control mechanism that includes an administrative frame very clear;

- has to present politics and processes to evaluate and administrate the operational risk exposures;

- has to make a proof of a recovery plan in case of different
  scenarios.

In this way, the financial institution is protected against losses during crisis. The financial institutions have at their disposal different instruments that they can use in the moment they decide to administrate the operational risk. These instruments are the evaluation and identification of risk; risk indexes; database of the events that generate losses; the risk plan or the target increase.

Banking Risk Management

The risk management is a managerial process that involves all the techniques and methods to evaluate and analyze the risk. It is represented by different processes such as measuring, controlling, reporting or choosing that decisions which lead to the reduction of all risks. In this way, they offer the bank a better vision regarding the future image or the politics and banking strategies that have to be developed.

Informer-Pay Net Group Romania proposes to banks a complete risk management solution to implement the Basel II Agreement regulations, as their representative, Cristian Artemi, declared: "Romania integration process into European financial market oblige the banks to adopt business strategies based on competitiveness. Informer Group sustains this process through permanent solutions that help the banks to pass easier from the basic approaches to the advanced ones and to generate real advantages like the loss reduction and capital pass in the reserve." Another company that developed solutions for the development of risk management is TLC Risk Solutions. They developed a complete solution, Barracuda. Its goal is to offer a coherent vision for the present or future positions regarding all the risks mentioned by the

Basel II Agreement and the National Financial Institution responsible with risk regulations and it gives the possibility to use all the approaches: basic approach, standard approach or advanced approach.

Through the Regulation 17/2003, the National Bank of Romania forced banks to improve their risk management systems. They have an obligation to evaluate the operations, the sensitive activities, and that exposure to this risk. The role of the banking management is to evaluate not only the institution risk exposure, but also the controlling methods and techniques of different risk situations.

The main objectives of the banking management are profitability maximization and risk exposure minimization. In case the company achieves this, employees become more serious and responsible for their job and also the psychological effect of not engaging in frauds is more powerful. In conclusion, the final goal and objective is to identify and eliminate the risks. But the identification of the risk factors, the evaluation, the control and the risk reduction are the main steps taken in the risk analysis and depend on the period of time considered, the costs and benefits, the data and information veracity, the possible externalities and interdependences between the events. The existence of proper programs to prevent and control the banking risks is of great importance for the name of the bank and its position in the market or different bank associations.

Present experience in Risk Management in Indian Banks

The regulatory initiatives as well as the banks' individual efforts in the direction of risk management have certainly improved the risk management standards in Indian banks in the past few years. Since, the initiation of structural reforms in the Indian banking sector in 1991, the reach and business volumes of Indian banks have increased two-fold; the operations have grown and assumed a higher degree of sophistication. The Indian banks' current capital base and liquidity position are broadly comfortable, as a starting point, *vis-à-vis* the Basel III guidelines. Both the CRAR (capital to risk-weighted assets ratio) and the core CRAR of Indian banks, respectively stood at 10.42 percent and 9.24 percent respectively on March 31, 1997, and have consistently remained well above the regulatory requirement of 9 percent and 6 percent, respectively under Basel II. The CRAR and core CRAR were at 13.88 percent and 9.7 percent respectively as at March 31, 2013. Indian banks, thus, start from a position of strength in the process of transition to the Basel III regime.

Many challenges, however, still lie ahead which will be delved into later in this paper. Asset quality is an important parameter to measure the health of the banks and concomitant with asset quality is the provisioning coverage that banks hold against stressed assets. Asset quality of the Indian banking system had improved significantly since the introduction of prudential norms, Securitization and Reconstruction of Financial Assets and Enforcement of Security Interest Act, 2002 (SARFAESI Act), Corporate Debt Restructuring (CDR) Mechanism, Credit Information Companies, etc. The GNPAs (Gross Non Performing Assets) ratio steadily declined from 15.7 percent in 1996-97 to 2.35 percent in 2010-11. However, due to the fallout of the global financial crisis and the consequent headwinds from many advanced nations in the west, the GNPAs have risen to 2.94 percent as on March 2012 and further to 3.42 percent as at the end of March 2013. As per the provisional data, as on December 2013, the GNPA ratio was at 4.47 percent. The ratio of restructured standard advances to gross advances stood at 5.8 percent at end-March 2013 adding to the total stress.

All Indian banks, including foreign banks in India, migrated to the standardized approaches of Basel II by March 31, 2009, in two phases. Large sized Indian banks and banks with an international presence have been encouraged to adopt the Basel II advanced approaches for computation of capital for credit, market and operational risk. Out of the 14 banks that submitted applications for migration to the Internal Rating Based approach for credit risk, seven have been given approval for parallel run. Under operational risk, parallel run has been approved for two banks for TSA (The Standardized Approach) out of the 13 banks that applied. Ten banks have so far conveyed their intent for migration to the AMA (Advanced Measurement Approach) of which cases of four large banks, which made preliminary submissions in this regard are under different stages of examination.

In respect to market risk, eight banks have conveyed their intent for migration to the Internal Model Approach. There is, however, another very significant aspect of the bank operations, just as in any corporate entity, and that is the commercial aspect viz., profitability management. Profitability in banks, as in the corporate, is reflective of the financial well-being, health and robustness of the entity and has a direct bearing on its capital formation ability. On the flip side, if the bank's strategies, business models, planning and operations and risk management are weak, obsolete or outdated or not in tune with the macroeconomic environment, the income flowing therefrom may be low or may end up in losses.

Profitability is impacted by the business decisions of the bank, the business model it pursues, quality and type of asset base as also by operational efficiencies and any noteworthy shift in its strategies and policies. The risk profile of a bank can also be gauged from its income and expenditure statement to a great extent. However, currently, the alignment of risk management and profitability management objectives are not so much in focus.

The profitability or the income and expenditure plans and decisions of the banks are directly connected to the regulatory concerns of capital adequacy. At the same time, solvency as the stability and soundness of banks, is also incumbent on the banks and the supervisors to carefully analyze the components of income and expenditure. A careful analysis and comparison of these streams of income and expenses would provide the bank an in-depth understanding of its business focus, structure and stability of profits and serve as the guiding principles for rebalancing and / restructuring its balance sheet. This would enable a bank to not only, derive optimum earnings, rationalize cost and expenses but also to initiate changes in and diversify its business design / model in alignment with the industry or the current and profitable market practices.

Process of operational risk management and recent trends

Through operational risk management, the bank wants to reduce the errors and improper activities that have a strong impact on the clients, financial losses or give a bad reputation to the company. If we select from the specialty literature Cummins, Lewis and Wei (2005), they presented four theories regarding operational risk management.

The opponents of the capital need for the operational risk considered that this type of risk can be easily diversified by the investors. In comparison with the other types of risk, operational risk is asymmetric and is strongly related to losses, not earnings. But the financial institutions can administrate the operational risk only to the point where the marginal expenses are equal to the reduction of marginal loss that appeared because of the events that generated operational losses.

The modern risk management theories consider that financial institutions can have earnings if they administer the risks because of some factors such as a convex form of taxes, financial costs and losses, asymmetric information or agents' costs.

Recent Global Initiatives in Banks for Strengthening Risk Management

In response to the global financial crisis, a package of reforms collectively referred to as Basel III (started in 2013 and with complete implementation schedule by 2019) was disseminated as part of the global regulatory effort to enhance the soundness and resilience of the banking system. These reforms focus on capital, liquidity, leverage and macro-prudential aspects of banking risk management. The Basel III, on the one hand, attempts to improve the quality and quantity of loss absorbing capital that a bank holds and aims at increasing the risk coverage of the capital framework, in particular for trading

activities, securitizations exposures to off-balance sheet vehicles and coun-
terparty credit exposures arising out of derivatives.

On the other hand, it has devised regulation for dealing with systemic risk
by prescribing countercyclical capital requirement, to contain pro-cyclicality
and a framework for a global list of systemically important banks (G-SIBs) and
domestic systemically important banks (D-SIBs) has also been laid down to
manage risks arising from inter-connectedness. The reforms require banks to
raise the amount of common equity to 4.5 percent of assets by January 2019
from the current 2 percent requirement under Basel II.

The innovative elements of the Basel III requirements include additional
layers of capital in the form of Capital Conservation Buffer and Countercyclical Capital Buffer, minimum Liquidity requirements in the form of short-term
Liquidity Coverage Ratio (LCR) and long-term structural Net Stable Funding
Ratio (NSFR), a leverage ratio as a back-stop to the risk-based capital framework and additional proposals for the Global Systemically Important Banks
(G-SIBs). The Capital Conservation Buffer is prescribed as 2.5 percent of
common equity in addition to the 4.5 percent minimum requirement bringing the total common equity requirements to 7 percent which if breached
would restrict pay-outs of earnings to help protect the minimum common
equity requirement. The capital buffer can be used to absorb losses during the
periods of financial and economic stress. The countercyclical capital buffer
entails common equity or other fully loss absorbing capital in the range of 0 to
2.5 percent to be implemented according to national circumstances and kicks
in when credit to GDP ratio deviates significantly from the trend.

The paradigm-changing approach to risk management under Basel III is introducing macro-prudential regulations to deal with systemic risk. The global
financial crisis brought home the point that even while individual financial
institutions are strong, when each of them acts to preserve its own interests,
these actions can lead to instability of the system. An internationally harmo-
nized leverage ratio has been introduced as a simple back-stop facility to
complement the risk-based capital framework in order to contain build-up of
excessive leverage in the system and comprises of 3 percent loss absorbing
capital relative to all of a bank's assets, including off-balance sheet assets
without risk weighting.

Current developments and Emerging Regulatory Scenario in India

for improving Risk Management in Banks

The Reserve Bank of India (RBI) has also adopted a proactive and calibrated
approach towards demanding and facilitating robust risk management efforts
by the Indian banks. RBI has been adopting a considered approach of limiting

the systemic risk originating from both the pro-cyclicality as well as interconnectedness dimensions. For example, countercyclical measures were adopted as early as 2004 to stall the heating up of certain sectors by increasing the risk weights and provisioning ratios for sensitive sectors such as capital market, housing, commercial real estate during the period when the boom was building up. RBI has been taking several measures to reduce the inter-connectedness among Indian banks, on the one hand, and between banks and non-banking financial companies (NBFCs) on the other, to address the cross-sectional dimension of systemic risk and regulatory limits have been placed on exposures to capital market exposures. Such a macro-prudential approach, which was not widely prevalent, then, saved the domestic economy from the adverse shocks during the height of the global financial crisis in 2008.

To meet the current compliance needs and prepare for the future, banks need to follow the five key imperatives for managing operational risk.

1. Changing regulations

2. Balancing cost with time to compliance

3. Integration of Finance and Risk functions

4. Building an enhanced data governance and risk reporting culture

5. Building strong model management capabilities – driven by technology, partner ecosystem, and in-house teams

The Way Ahead

Over the years and especially in the wake of the learning from the global financial crisis, banks have enhanced their efforts in the direction of improving risk management practices. However, going forward much work still remains, which includes:

a) Banks must pay greater attention to the risk governance aspects, wherein the boards must have a full understanding of the risks, typical to the respective bank as also full involvement in designing appropriate policies and strategies for the risk management. For this purpose, risk appetite and risk tolerance levels must be clearly defined, keeping a past and forward looking view on likely internal and external risk environment.

b)   An independent risk management function is headed by a
     CRO (Chief Risk Officer) with sufficient freedom and stature
     assumes critical importance. Banks must ensure that the
     board level risk committees as also the independent chal-
     lenge functioning in the form of internal and external audit /
     reviews are effective in the real sense and have the requisite
     understanding, resources and wherewithal to perform their
     responsibility in a meaningful way.

c)   Senior management of the banks must play a proactive role.
     They should communicate the risk management policies, risk
     appetite and tolerance statement, risk management practices
     to the operational in-charges at the business units and corpo-
     rate levels for proper understanding and compliance. These
     efforts need to be supplemented by a robust MIS (Manage-
     ment Information System) and information technology plat-
     forms to provide its stake holders with timely, reliable and
     complete risk-related information on the bank for effective
     decision making and decisive action taking.

d)   Use tests which entail the use of inputs and outputs from the
     quantitative models in enhancing quality risk management and
     decision-making need better encouragement. Over-reliance on
     quantitative models can have grossly under-estimate tail risks
     and it is necessary to also use expert judgment in dealing with
     risk estimation and management. Stress tests, as also reverse
     stress tests and back testing, should be gainfully utilized as
     complements to model based risk estimation.

Conclusion

The banks can manage the banking risks only if they admit the strategic role
of administrating the risk, if they use the paradigm analyze-management in
order to increase the efficiency, if they adopt precise measures to adjust the
performance to risk and, of course, if they will create mechanisms to report
performance. Nowadays, a lot of companies make the differences between
the risks that can be controlled and the ones that do not. The controlled risks
are the risks where the bank's activities can influence the result and they can
be covered normally, without the need of a third party. The uncontrolled risks
are represented by the risks that cannot be internally controlled by the bank.
For example, they can be covered against the natural catastrophes through
insurance from an insurance company.

References

Bennett, A. (2017). Currency Strategies to Minimize Costs and Mitigate Risks in the Aviation Industry, Credit Control, p.48.

Bolton, N. and Berkey, J. (2005). Aligning Basel II Operational Risk and Sarbanes- Oxley 404 Projects. In E. Davis (Ed.), Operational Risk: Practical Approaches to Implementation. London: Risk Books.

Breden, D. (2008). Monitoring the Operational Risk Environment Effectively. Journal of Risk Management in Financial Institutions, 1, 156–164.

Copeland, J. "Operational Risk Management (ORM)" - WR-ALC / SES.

Coyle, B. (2000). Hedging Currency Exposures: Currency Risk Management, Financial World Publications, UK, 17-18.

Fheili, M. I. (2007). Employee turnover: An HR risk with firm-specific context. Journal of Operations Risk Management, 2, 69–84.

Fung, W. and Hsieh, D. A. (2004), Hedge Funds Bench Marks - A Risk Based Approach, Journal of Financial Analysts, 58(5) 65-80.

Kanthi Gosh, S. Measures of reputation risk, Dec 8th 2011, Financial Express.

Peccia, A. (2003). Using Operational Risk Models to Manage Operational Risk. In C. Alexander (Ed.), Operational Risk: Regulation, Analysis and Management, London: Prentice Hall-Financial Times.

Prindl, A.R. (1976). Foreign Exchange Risk, Wiley, London.

Rao, V. and Dev, A. (2006). Operational Risk: Some Issues in Basel II AMA Implementation in US Financial Institutions. In E. Davis (Ed.), The Advanced Measurement Approach to Operational Risk, London: Risk Books.

Tushar, A. (2017). Explaining the sharp rise in the Rupee. The Business Line, 28th Mar.

Chapter 9

Foreign Exchange Risk Management Practices in Commercial Banks of India

Koneru Kusuma,
Assistant Professor,
GITAM Institute of Management,
GITAM University.

V.Gowri Lakshmi,
Assistant Professor,
GITAM Institute of Management,
GITAM University.

Introduction

The process of globalization has accelerated. From the beginning of the 21st century, India has witnessed a significant shift from an inward –looking development strategy concentrating on import substitution to a more open economy. Foreign direct and portfolio investments are on the rise. The legal framework for administration of foreign exchange transactions in India is provided by Foreign Exchange Management Act, 1999 (FEMA came into force on June 1, 2000). The role of commercial banks in foreign exchange risk management: they should merge their money market and foreign exchange operations treat it as a separate profit centre for better efficiency, foreign exchange derivatives market contracts, overseas commodity, freight hedging, rupee accounts of nonresident banks, interbank foreign exchange dealings are governed by the provisions in notifications. Foreign exchange risk management primarily tries to mitigate the exchange rate risk arising out on the risk of investments value changing due to the changes in currency exchange rates. This risk usually affects exporters /importers / investors making international investments; the guidelines are enunciated in the master circular on risk management and interbank dealings issued by foreign exchange department of RBI as amended and issued in July 2011.

Foreign exchange is the conversion of one country's currency to another. Also, a country's currency can be pegged to another currency. The value of any particular currency is determined by market forces based on geo-political risk /tourism investment and trade; all these requirements produce a need for foreign exchange and foreign exchange market emerged on a large scale. Foreign exchange is handled globally between banks. The foreign exchange market is a global decent realized or OTC market for the trading of currencies. This market determines foreign exchange rate; the main participants in this market are the larger international banks, financial institutions, and banks turn to a smaller number of financial firms known as dealers involved in large quantities of foreign exchange trading. Most of the foreign exchange dealers are banks; this is called the "inter-bank market".

Methodology

This study uses relevant material collected from various journals, research papers, magazines, textbooks, government-recognized web pages. This study uses secondary data to answer the research questions.

Literature Review

This literature review gives us an insight into the importance of foreign exchange risk management, various categories of currency risk and various techniques used to manage foreign exchange risks.

Epstein (2003) observes and reveals an assessment of experiences from the 1990s and lessons for the future. The capital management technique term refers to two complementary types of financial policies: 1) policies that govern international capital flows and 2) policies that enforce prudential management of domestic financial institutions. The most important lesson from this paper is capital management techniques that enhance overall financial and current stability efficacy. But all countries cannot use the same techniques.

Das and Ghosh (2005) investigate the performance of Indian commercial banking sector during the post-reform period 1992-2002 with three different approaches namely intermediate approach, value–added approach and operating approach. These approaches have been employed to differentiate how efficiency scores vary with changes in inputs and outputs. The findings suggest that medium–sized public sector banks performed reasonably well and are more likely to operate at higher levels of technical efficiency.

Berger (2007) reviews the research in three areas namely the comparison of the efficiency of banks in different nature with all banks measured against a common frontier, the comparison of the efficiency of banks in different nations with banks from each nation measured against their own nation–specific frontier and the comparisons of the efficiency of foreign owned versus domestically owned banks with both types of banks measured against the same nation specific frontier. The author after making a perfect comparison believes that value added is greatest.

Leyla Ahmed (Nov, 2015) specifies the fact that common banks deal in foreign currencies by holding assets and liabilities in foreign denominated currencies. They are continuously exposed to foreign exchange risk. Forex of a common bank comes from its very trade and non-trade services.

Foreign exchange is not only the impact of adverse exchange rate movements on the earnings of the bank due to different open positions held, but it is also the impact on the earnings and capital of bank in different ways. Forex also exposes a bank interest rate risk. Banks pose a serious risk of default to the Forex transactions which can lead to time zone risk and sovereign or country risk.

Foreign currency exchange risk is the additional riskiness or variance of a firm's cash flows that may be attributed to currency fluctuations. All major sources of hard currencies of international transactions are sources of foreign exchange risk to common banks in Kenya. Even though there are a number of techniques such as in Forex, the practical relevance is these techniques are too sophisticated and difficult to implement in developing countries.

Debasish's (2008) study covers a sample of 501 corporate falling in 18 different categories, and cited 53 percent of the respondents are using derivatives, nonusers of derivates are into currency risk, next in importance being interest rate risk and marginally equity risk, greatest preference is for simple forward contracts.

Foreign exchange markets

There is no organized exchange where foreign exchange can be traded. Foreign exchange markets consisting of banks globally are over-the counter (OTC) markets. Foreign exchange markets are in operation all the time. Foreign exchange transactions are primarily conducted during banking hours, some centres are always open for the sake of banks constituted globally. The communication medium is SWIFT (Society for Worldwide Inter-Bank Financial Transactions), a Belgian non-cooperative society connecting all major banks and centers with one another. ISO has developed a unique three-letter code for each of the world currencies to have clarity in communication.

Forex market is bifurcated into two transactions, transactions within the banks are called inter-bank transactions, and the transactions between the banker and their customers are known as merchant bank transactions.

Foreign exchange risk

Risk management helps to reduce the probability of lapping bad things and increases the frequency of happening good things.

Foreign exchange risk is also known as FX risk. Exchange rate risk or currency risk is a financial risk of an investments value changing due to the changes in currency exchange rates. An asset or investment dominated in foreign currency loses its value, any changes in the currency exchange rate will cause that investments value will change when the investment is sold and converted back into the original currency.

According to the BIS (Bank for International Settlement), the preliminary global results from 2016 triennial central bank survey of foreign exchange and OTC derivatives market activity shows that trading in foreign exchange markets averaged to $ 5.09 trillion per day in April 2016.

As per RBI foreign exchange turnover data on 23rd October 2017the spot merchant /interbank sales amounted to 1,720 million dollars. The exchange of the Indian rupee is a worldwide network of inter-bank traders consisting of the principal players, banks, and other major participants such as the government, interbank brokerage houses exchange companies, travelers.

The inter-bank market is called as wholesale market, whereas travelers, individuals and tourists make up the retail market.

Exchange rate refers to the price paid in one currency to acquire one unit of foreign currency or receive foreign currency by selling one unit of currency.

Exchange rate regimes

An exchange rate is the value of one currency in terms of another. The term exchange rate regime refers to determining exchange rates at a point of time and the changes over time including the factors responsible for change. At one end exchange rates are rigid or fixed, and on the other end they are perfectly flexible or floating exchange rates, spanning them are hybrids with varying degrees of limited flexibility.

The world has experienced three different exchange rate regimes in this country starting from the global standard regime of fixed rates, passing through the adjustable peg system after the World War-II it finally ended up with a system of managed floats. Since 1985, the unified exchange rate phase has witnessed improvement in informational and operational efficiency of the foreign exchange market, at a hailing price. (Satya Swaroop Debashish, 1996).

Exchange rate regimes-the current scenario

IMF classifies member countries into 8 categories based on the exchange rate regime adopted by them. The first category is the exchange arrangement between the countries of a currency union, (countries which share common currency), 15 members of EMU (Economic &Monetary Union) who developed the Euro as their common currency in Africa. For example, Central African Economic & Monetary Union which has Cameroon, Central African Republic Chad as its members.

The Australian dollar used by Kiribati, Nauru and Tuvalu Andorra, Kosova and Montenegro use the Euro as their legal tender even though they are not the members of European Union. A regime under legislative commitment, conventional fixed peg arrangements, pegged exchange rates with horizontal bands crawling peg, crawling bands managed floating with no pre announced path for the exchange rate independently floating.

Foreign exchange risk arises when a bank holds assets and liabilities in foreign currencies and impacts the earnings and capital of the bank due to the fluctuations in the exchange rates. The exchange rate can move upward or down in the next period this uncertain movement poses a threat to the earnings and capital of the bank if the movement is in an unanticipated direction.

Foreign exchange risk can be either transactional or translational. Transactional risk arises due to transactions in foreign currencies and can be hedged using different techniques. Translational risk is an accounting risk arising because of translation of assets held in foreign currency or abroad.

Foreign exchange risk in commercial banks

Commercial banks actively deal in foreign currencies holding assets and liabilities in foreign denominated currencies are continuously exposed to foreign exchange risk foreign exchange risk of a commercial bank comes from its very trade and non-trade services.

The types of risks to which a bank is particularly exposed in its operations are liquidity risk, credit risk, market risks, exposure risks and investment risks. Risks relating to the country of origin of the entity to which a bank is exposed are operational risk, legal risk, reputational risk and strategic risk. Foreign exchange risk comes under market risk which also includes interest rate causes negative effects on the financial results and capital of the bank.

Foreign exchange trading activities include (Saunders & Cornett, 2003) the purchase and sale of foreign currencies to partake in and complete international commercial trade transactions.

Customers or financial institutions will purchase and sell foreign currencies to take positions in foreign real and financial investment.

The purchase and sale of foreign currencies for hedging purposes is aimed at reducing exposure in any currency.

When transactions are done on behalf half of the customer the risk is transferred to the customer, the bank here plays only an agency role. If the bank opts for hedging, no risk will be more in speculative purposes which may result in the gain or loss due to an unexpected outcome.

Spot, forward and swap are the principal FX related contracts; the banking products and services in foreign exchange give rise to non-traded foreign currency exposure.

Foreign currency exposure of a commercial bank

The unhedged position in a particular currency gives rise to FX risk and is an open position in that particular currency. The banks maintain two positions, namely net short and net long positions.

If a bank sells more foreign currency than it has purchased, it is said to be in a net short position. If a bank purchases more foreign currency than it has sold then it is said to be in a net long position. Foreign currency may fall in value compared to local or home currency and becomes a reason for substantial loss for a bank if it is in the net long position; both the positions are exposed to risk if the foreign currency falls in value when compared to local or home currency.

A long position is also known as overbought or net asset position and a short position is also known as a net liability or oversold position. The sum of all the net assets positions and net liabilities positions are known as net open position or net foreign currency exposure. The negative unhedged position of a bank shows a net short position whereas a positive figure shows a net open position of foreign currencies in a bank.

Foreign exchange risk management

The foreign currency transactions are done by commercial banks on behalf of customers. When the transactions are on behalf of customer, the risk is transferred to the customer and there is no risk to the bank. The bank's assets and liabilities in foreign currencies or assets and liabilities in other countries give rise to foreign exchange risk which has to be managed by the bank; the bank will be exposed to the risk of exchange rate, whenever a commercial bank deals in foreign currency.

Foreign exchange risk management strategies and techniques

Hedging strategies and techniques

Foreign currency risk is mitigated by hedging techniques. Hedging eliminates or minimizes its risk exposure, Hedging in Indian commercial banks can be as follows.

- Foreign currency assets and liabilities match

- Hedging using derivatives.

- Hedging through diversification of foreign asset-liability portfolio

- Risk sharing

- Natural Hedging

- Matching and Netting

- Leading and lagging

Risk sharing: Both buyers and sellers intend to stay in a long relationship whether it is a banking business or any other business. In international transactions of business, this relationship should not destroy because of volatile foreign exchange rates. In this context, both the seller and buyer bank agree to share the currency risk.

Natural Hedging: The most popular method to mitigate currency exchange risk is the simple natural hedge when exporter and importer complete a transaction in the same currency. A natural hedge is the reduction in risk that can arise from institutions normal operating procedures. Banks involved in international trade. Often attempt to match the currency denomination of their receipts and payments in order to limit foreign exchange exposure.

Matching and Netting: Netting and matching is a feature of foreign exchange risk management. They are carried out to reduce the scale of external hedging required, and netting refers to netting off group receipts and payments. Matching extends this concept to include third parties to banks, banks can reduce the size of their counter party exposures by entering into legally binding agreements to net settlements bilaterally, and netting arrangements permit banks to offset trade against each other So only net amount in each currency is paid or received by each institution.

Leading and lagging: Leading and lagging helps to take advantage of exchange rate swings by adjusting payments. They are aggressive foreign exchange tactics and a strategy of shifting funds from weak currency to a strong currency. At the time of payment, if the importer expects that the currency due to receive will depreciate attempts shall be made to delay payment by exceeding the credit terms. On the other hand, if the exporter expects that the currency due to be received will depreciate, attempts will be made to obtain payment immediately, by offering a discount for immediate payment. The premature payment for goods purchased is called the lead and delayed payment is called a lag.

Hedging using derivatives

- Forwards

- Futures

- Swaps

- Options

Forwards: Transactions in foreign currency can be either in spot or forwards depending upon the time of settlement, if the transactions are to be settled immediately then they are termed as spot transactions. Transactions in foreign currency can also be made for settlement at a later date such transactions where the rates are fixed straight away, but the exchange of currency is set for a later date are known as forward contracts. In an option when a forward specific date is not given, a forward contract can be booked for delivery within a given period.

Forward contracts are suitable for covering foreign exchange risks for short periods. In India, forwards are not allowed beyond a specific maturity period of six months for the contracts of long duration roll over forwards are generally used.

Swap: A swap transaction is a combination of spot and forward transactions and consists of both the forward and spot legs of the swap are opposite and are equal in value. The rates for buying spot and selling forward would be different the bank would not be exposed to any risk of fluctuating exchange rates.

Central bank role in foreign exchange risk management

Central bank intervention is necessary because of the importance of the capital flows in determining exchange rate movements as against trade balances and economic growth. Capital flows are volatile exposing financial market to risk to curtail this central bank intervention is necessary, all the commercial banks are given guidelines by the central bank to be followed continuously to achieve the financial stability in their respective economies. The intervention of the central bank can be sterilized and non-sterilized.

The RBI publishes half-yearly reports on the management of foreign exchange reserves for bringing about more transparency and enhancing the level of disclosure. The foreign exchange reserves stood at USD 372.0 billion on September 2016. By the end of October 2016, these reserves decreased to USD 361.1 billion as at the end of November 2016. The funds further decreased to USD 358.9 billion on December 2016, and subsequently in January and February of 2017 the reserves increased.

Although USD and Euro can be used as intervention currencies, FCA is maintained in USD. The movements in FCA occur mainly on account of the purchase and sale of foreign exchange by RBI, the income arising out of the deployment of the foreign exchange reserves, the external and receipt of the central government and the changes on account of revaluation of assets.

Conclusion

Risk management has gained more importance on account of the increased globalization of financial markets. The benefits of the increased flow of capital between nations include a better international allocation of capital between nations and greater opportunities to diversify risk. Globalization of investment is meant for new risks from exchange rates, political actions, and increased interdependence on financial conditions of different countries.

The advent of globalization has witnessed a rapid rise in the quantum of cross-border flows involving different currencies, posing challenges to the shift from low-risk to high –risk operations in foreign exchange transactions. Reduction in the volatility of cash flows is the main reason for hedging.

References

Abor, J. (2005). Managing foreign exchange risk among Ghanaian firms. Journal of Risk Finance, 6(4),306-318.

Ahmed, L. (2015). "The effect of foreign exchange exposure on the financial performance of commercial banks in Kenya, International Journal of Scientific &Research Publications, 5(11).

Baillie, R.T. and McMohan, P.C (1989). The Foreign Exchange Market Theory and Econometric Evidence. Cambridge. Cambridge University Press.

Bernanke, B. S. and Gertler, M. (2001). "Should Central Banks Respond to Movements in Asset Prices?" American Economic Review, 91(2), 253-257

Cooper, D. R and Schindler, P. S (2006). Business Research Methods.New Delhi, Tata Mc. Graw Hill.

Das, A. and Ghosh. S (2005). Financial deregulation & efficiency: An empirical analysis of Indian banks during the post reform period, Review of Financial Economics, The University of New Orleans.

Davis N. and Kutan, A.M. (2003). Inflation and output as predictors of stock returns and volatility, international evidence. Applied Financial Economics, 13(9), 693-700.

Epstein, G. et al. (2003), "Capital Management Techniques in Developing Countries: An Assessment of Experiences from the 1990s and lessons for the Future".

He, L.E., Fayman, A. and Casey, M.S. (2014). Bank profitability: "The impact of foreign currency fluctuations. Journal of Applied Business and Economics, 16(2), 14-20.

Shastri, K.Q. and Tandon, K. (2009). "Valuation of Currency Options: Some Empirical tests. Journal of Financial and Quantitative Analysis, 21(2), 145-160.

Swaroop Debasish, S. (2008). Foreign Exchange Risk net practices – A study in Indian scenario. BRAC University Journal, V (2), 81-91.

Vander Linden, D. (2014). "Is hedging foreign currency bids with options desirable? An applied analysis for small firms. Journal of Applied Financial Research, 19.

Index

R

Retail Clients, 37
risk hedging, xxiv
Risk sharing, 107

S

SEBI, 2

V

Variance Decomposition, 59

W

WTO, 4

www.ingramcontent.com/pod-product-compliance
Lightning Source LLC
Chambersburg PA
CBHW061329220326
41599CB00026B/5103